THE
SECRETS OF
SPIRITUAL
HEALING

THE SECRETS OF SPIRITUAL HEALING

An Hachette UK Company
www.hachette.co.uk

Summersdale Publishers Ltd
Part of Octopus Publishing Group Limited
Carmelite House
50 Victoria Embankment
LONDON
EC4Y 0DZ
UK

www.summersdale.com

Printed and bound in Poland

ISBN: 978-1-78783-683-9

Substantial discounts on bulk quantities of Summersdale books are available to corporations, professional associations and other organizations. For details contact general enquiries: telephone: +44 (0) 1243 771107 or email: enquiries@summersdale.com.

DISCLAIMER
The author and the publisher cannot accept responsibility for any misuse or misunderstanding of any information contained herein, or any loss, damage or injury, be it health, financial or otherwise, suffered by any individual or group acting upon or relying on information contained herein. None of the views or suggestions in this book is intended to replace medical opinion from a doctor who is familiar with your particular circumstances. If you have concerns about your health, please seek professional advice.

The Dum

Dales

40 favourite Walks

The authors and publisher have made every effort to ensure that the information in this publication is accurate, and accept no responsibility whatsoever for any loss, injury or inconvenience experienced by any person or persons whilst using this book.

published by
pocket mountains ltd
The Old Church, Annanside,
Moffat DG10 9HB

ISBN: 978-1-907025-70-9

A catalogue record for this book is available from the British Library

Contains Ordnance Survey data © Crown copyright and database 2018 supported by out of copyright mapping 1945-1961

Printed in Poland

Introduction

From Nithsdale in the west, through Annandale at its heart and Eskdale in the east, Dumfriesshire's three dales remain, despite the bustle of modern life, an accessible rural idyll. Each comes complete with a namesake river rising in the dale's northern hills, meandering through mid-point undulations, on over the flat lowlands to eventually meet with the mighty tides of the Solway Firth. This is a place to don your walking boots and take to the rolling hills and quiet backroads or hop, skip and jump the tidal gullies of the Solway merse.

Each of these 40 walks explores much of what makes Dumfriesshire a great outdoors destination and although never far from civilisation (Glasgow, Edinburgh and Carlisle are all within easy reach), many of these walks are infused with a feeling of being in the middle of nowhere.

History

This is border country, where the accessible dales conveniently connected Scotland and England via logical 'highways' much used by marauding forces from both sides through the ages as bloody skirmishes became the norm. The Romans set up camps across the area (yes, they did get further than Hadrian's Wall!), while in later centuries many a regal visitor, complete with army, passed this way. Robert Bruce, King of Scots, hails from these parts, and Edward I of England – the Hammer of the Scots – invaded and built a mighty castle at Lochmaben, the same castle where King James V of Scotland later mustered his forces before attacking England.

Even when war subsided, daily life was still dangerous. Border parishes flip-flopped between Scottish and English control and a whole region – the Debatable Lands – was set aside as a buffer zone where permanent settlement was not allowed. Mercenary freebooters known as 'reivers' (most famously the Armstrong clan) did move in, however, and a lawless no-man's land ensued, particularly in the area from Carlisle up to Langholm, where robbing, plundering and even murder was commonplace. Finally, after the Union of the Crowns in 1603, King James VI of Scotland stamped his authority over the reivers by hanging the worst offenders and exiling the rest to Ireland and the Low Countries.

Centuries-long loyalty to the winning monarchs of the day saw the gradual emergence of large estates, many of which still exist. One of Britain's largest private landowners, the Duke of Buccleuch and Queensberry, has estates in Nithsdale, Eskdale and beyond, and many of the walks in this volume roam these lands.

The Victorians flocked to the area in their droves, alighting at 'Beattock for Moffat' train station to immerse themselves in the 'health-giving' spa waters. Love-struck couples, meanwhile, raced up the Carlisle Road from England,

often hotly pursued by angry parents, to wed at Gretna Green.

A diverse range of religious influences is seen all around, from the ancient through to the unexpected. Early stone circles can be discovered just a stone's throw from Dumfries, 7th-century monastic remains sit on the banks of the River Annan, while in the upper reaches of the Esk are the temple and stupas of Samye Ling, the first Tibetan Buddhist Centre in the West.

The Dumfriesshire Dales have borne many famous sons (although seemingly fewer daughters), including Robert the Bruce (King of Scots), Henry Duncan (theologian/social reformer), Thomas Telford (engineer), Thomas Carlyle (essayist), and more recently Hugh MacDiarmid (poet) and Calvin Harris (music producer). For Robert Burns, Scotland's national bard, these dales became in later life his home, workplace and muse. For female inspiration, there's Jane Haining, from Nithsdale who, in trying to protect her charges, became the only Scots woman to die in Auschwitz.

Wildlife and topography

The joy of walking these dales comes in the sheer range of wildlife and landscapes over a compact area, roughly 60km from top to bottom. In the morning explore craggy hills with glacial lakes and heather-clad uplands, while after lunch wander through lush flower-filled pasture, see the tidal bore rush up the estuary and taste the salty air of the Solway Firth.

The county has its fair share of rarities, but even the most common species can bring interest: an orange tip butterfly in spring, the drum of a great-spotted woodpecker, or a circling buzzard. Harder to spot, but rewarding if seen, are the playful antics of otters – try the caul (weir) in Dumfries or Lochmaben's Castle Loch, mighty osprey along Moffat Water, starling murmurations near Gretna, agile red squirrels at Eskrigg, or the silent daytime hunting of short-eared owl and regal flutter of emperor moth over the moorlands. In winter, when the snowy higher-level walks are the preserve of more experienced walkers, the Solway Firth becomes a hive of activity with feeding barnacle and pink-footed geese, along with the honking call of whooper swans.

One big change in recent decades has been the commercial afforestation of hillsides with sitka, while a more industrial 'afforestation' has evolved in the form of wind turbines – some love it, others less so!

Walking, weather and safety

Despite being only a short hop from Carlisle and barely an hour's drive from Glasgow and Edinburgh, the area remains surprisingly underexplored. Yet many of these routes might be walked without meeting another soul and while 'honeypots' do exist they are the exception rather than the rule.

Dumfriesshire weather is generally mild, if at times a bit rainy and changeable, even in winter, which is why migrating birds

flock here. Winter snows linger on higher ground well into spring and late frosts are not uncommon. Spring often arrives later than in other parts of the UK, while the year-round high precipitation leaves a permanently verdant countryside – it's rare to find a parched summer landscape here.

All route descriptions are written for year-round walking; however, walking at higher levels through fog or winter snows should only be undertaken by those with the experience and ability to use a map and compass (don't rely on mobile phones). At any time, an outlook of blue skies and sunshine can quickly turn to thick mist, rain or sleet, despite the forecasts. With this in mind it's advisable to carry warm and waterproof clothing, a drink and plenty to snack on, plus seriously consider taking a whistle, first aid kit and any medication, in case of delay.

Travel

Dumfriesshire can be tricky to navigate by bus or train to the more isolated spots. Buses tend to fan out from Dumfries and might not be frequent, so check in advance and, if required, arrange any taxi rides home before setting out as mobile coverage can be patchy. A useful website is www.dumgal.gov.uk/timetables.

Many routes start from a small village, beside a kirk or in a lay-by where parking considerately is the order of the day. If an event is on at a hall or kirk and the car park is busy, please look elsewhere for a space. Take care not to block farm gates,

do pay for tickets where required, and try to be generous in supporting rural communities by visiting the local shops.

About this guide

All of the walks are designed with some sort of focal point or purpose in mind: ancient ruins, wildlife, fine views or places with historical footprints.

Walks range from 3.5km to 16km and are generally a maximum of 3–4 hours, with these rough timings based on covering about 3.5km per hour, plus wiggle room for harder terrain.

The five chapters essentially follow the river catchment areas for each dale, separating out the hillier areas in the north from the more lowland reaches. The illustrative maps for each route are designed to be used in conjunction with the relevant OS Explorer (1:25,000) map, listed with each route.

The passing of The Land Reform (Scotland) Act in 2003 secured the traditional 'freedom to roam' in Scotland that had already been enjoyed, provided it is done responsibly, as set out in the Scottish Outdoor Access Code – details are at www.outdooraccess-scotland.scot.

This is farming and shooting country, upland areas are full of grazing sheep or grouse-shooting moors, lower areas often have cattle, while wildfowling takes place on the merse. Dogs need to be kept under control and on a lead through fields of livestock, sensitive wildlife habitats or where signs advise.

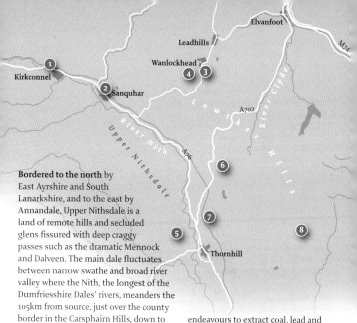

Bordered to the north by East Ayrshire and South Lanarkshire, and to the east by Annandale, Upper Nithsdale is a land of remote hills and secluded glens fissured with deep craggy passes such as the dramatic Mennock and Dalveen. The main dale fluctuates between narrow swathe and broad river valley where the Nith, the longest of the Dumfriesshire Dales' rivers, meanders the 105km from source, just over the county border in the Carsphairn Hills, down to the Solway Firth.

This is an area with a feel all of its own, one step removed from the mainstream. The largest town, the Royal Burgh of Sanquhar, proud and historic, sits at the foot of the Lowther Hills yet perched high enough above the Nith to keep out of harm's way, surveying a diverse scene of both the wild and the pastoral. All around is a landscape peppered with lonely farm steadings, hamlets and numerous castles both habitable and ruined. Sprinkle in Roman roads with fortlet remains, the world's oldest working post office, an historic tomb complete with dramatic *baldacchino* (canopy) atop four barley twist columns and the scars of man's endeavours to extract coal, lead and precious metals from beneath the soil, and you have an intriguing mix of contrasts.

A bloody history of religious persecution stains this now placid landscape. A period of struggle between the Scottish Presbyterians and English Episcopalians, enflamed by the Sanquhar Declarations, became chillingly known as 'The Killing Time'. Many Covenanters lost their lives during these 17th-century troubles and, to this day, tombs, markers and memorials are found throughout the area.

Today life is more peaceful and the Lowther Hills offer temptingly quiet but spectacular walking. But whatever you do, don't underestimate the changeable weather, particularly during the winter.

Drumlanrig Castle ▶

Upper Nithsdale

Kirkconnel and St Conal's Kirk

Distance 8km **Time** 2 hours 30
Terrain rough tracks, farm fields and
quiet roads **Map** OS Explorer 328
Access parking on Main Street or by the
kirk; buses from Dumfries; train station
at Kirkconnel

Kirkconnel's quiet lanes wriggle through
a patchwork of fields crisscrossed with
drystane dykes and full of munching
sheep. With an ambience of the 'dales' as
one imagines them – remote, authentic
and wild – the route takes in tumbling
waterfalls, one of southern Scotland's
oldest kirk sites and the pretty valley of
the Polbower Burn.

Heading west along Main Street, the
road climbs and curves around the parish
church. Completed in 1731, it's the final
resting place of Alexander Anderson, local
railwayman by day, poet by night, who
went on to become the chief librarian
of Edinburgh University. Just after the
church take the road on the right and
follow it for about 2km northwards
towards the distant hills.

Pass the 'Old Church Walk' parking
area on the right, stopping to peruse the
information boards: one tells the story
of the original church, while the other
explains the importance of coal to this
area, including the curious fact that the
first coal was gathered by monks who
lived at a nearby leper colony.

When the tarmac road ends at Old
Kirkland take the track on the right and
make your way around the plantation to
avoid walking through the yard at
Kirkland Farm. Rejoin the track beyond
the farm and follow it uphill and around
the back of Vennel cottage.

Cross the ford and continue over the

large wooden stile for a linear section up to one of the lesser known of Dumfriesshire's Greymare's Tail waterfalls. Keep to the burn's left bank, shadowing the fenceline up the steep section, then take the path dropping down to the water – follow your nose along here to the base of the waterfall (not many boots pass this way so there isn't an obvious path). This sheltered gully makes a perfect picnic spot before retracing your steps to the main route.

Once back over the stile, turn right, cross another ford and head on past the stone sheep pens to the remains of St Conal's Kirk. Situated close to a long-lost drovers' route, today the site stands isolated, weather-beaten and brimming with history dating back to the 9th century. Little remains from that time: the earliest dated grave marker is 1611, while the most prominent feature is the cairn commemorating the help of miners excavating this site during the 1926 General Strike.

Turn right on leaving the kirkyard and follow the drystane dyke to Glenwharrie cottage, at which point join the obvious gravel track and pass through the conifer plantation on the way back to Old Kirkland.

Retrace your steps to the parking area with the information boards passed earlier, then take the footpath off to the left along the wood edge, following it

down to the waters of the Polbower Burn, known locally as Baker's Burn as it once powered the local mill. Meander down the valley, crossing numerous bridges and climbing up over steep cuttings before dropping back to the burn. On a warm day this is the perfect spot to dangle your feet in the refreshing waters and watch the dippers.

On reaching the cottages, go through the gate and on under the railway to return to Kirkconnel's Main Street.

◄ Crossing Glenalymer Burn

9

Sanquhar and the Multiverse

Distance **11km** Time **3 hours 30**
Terrain **footpaths and quiet roads**
Maps **OS Explorer 328 and 329**
Access **town centre car parks; buses from Dumfries; train station at Sanquhar**

Situated at the foot of the Lowther Hills, Sanquhar's fortunes have waxed and waned with the centuries. Granted its Royal Charter in 1598, it played an important role in Scotland's 17th-century religious turmoil and became known for its coalmines and cottage weaving industry. Today the town offers an interesting mix of rural life, outdoor tourism and 'out-of-this-world' art, an ideal start to a walk of quiet backroads, burns and woodland.

Start by the impressive 18th-century Tolbooth, designed by Robert Adam and once the town jail, where the jougs that shackled wrongdoers to the outer wall remain. Today it houses a fascinating little museum: the perfect Sanquhar introduction. Passing to the right of the Tolbooth, cross over and take Church Road heading out of town and gently uphill behind the school.

At Crawick Water cross the footbridge, turning right along the road, and walk under the railway arch to Sanquhar's newest attraction. Located in an old open-cast mine, Crawick Multiverse is a massive installation exploring the universe, designed by internationally celebrated landscape artist and local resident Charles Jencks. Free to explore, there are a couple of suggested routes around the site on the information board by the entrance.

When you've come back down to earth, continue along the road and take the signed footpath off to the right. Pass in front of a cottage and carry on down to the Crawick Water to cross the zigzagging footbridges over the delightful Sodgers' Pool, named after the captured soldiers of

◀ Crawick Multiverse

Napoleon's army who once bathed here.

Taking the stepped uphill path, turn right on joining the road and follow it downhill for about 1.5km back to town. This stretch offers fine Nithsdale views and, for animal lovers in search of diversion, passes Clark's Little Ark animal sanctuary. Cross the railway and carry on down to the High Street, a few metres from the start point. Turn left along the street and continue out to the edge of town, passing the world's oldest working post office (since 1712) and an obelisk marking the pinning of the Sanquhar Declarations to the old town cross in 1680. This was a key act of defiance by the Scottish Presbyterians objecting to English Episcopalian interference during the bloody period known as 'The Killing Time'.

Cross the road to join the long-distance Southern Upland Way (SUW) for around 2km. Skirt to the right of the ruins of Sanquhar Castle, built by the Duke of Buccleuch but vacant since 1690, having been usurped by nearby Drumlanrig Castle, and continue along the raised bank around the houses. By the council depot the path leads you down to the River Nith.

Cross Blackaddie Bridge and then, turning immediately left, follow the road to Euchan Bridge. Here, leave the SUW and turn right to wander along the pretty Euchan Water. On the way take a little sip of the iron-rich waters at the well, look out for the earthworks of Kemp's Castle and pause high above tumbling Euchan Falls.

The path eventually curves away from the water. At the road turn right and follow it back to Blackaddie Bridge, crossing over and then turning right to take the road back up into town.

Wanlockhead to East Mount Lowther

Distance 8km **Time** 2 hours 30
Terrain footpaths, hard-surface track and
open hills **Map** OS Explorer 329
Access parking in Wanlockhead village;
bus from Sanquhar

Nestling in a hollow within the
Lowther Hills, Wanlockhead sits at 467m
above sea level and can proudly make
claim to be Scotland's highest village.
Starting your walk in such a lofty
position means ever more impressive
views for each metre climbed. This route
uses a mix of hard-surfaced access tracks
for the hilltop 'golf ball' radar station and
rough grassy hill paths, which can be
very exposed to wind and inclement
weather, so come prepared for all
eventualities, even in summer.

Owing its existence to man's
determination to extract the bounty of
precious metals and minerals found in
the surrounding hills, Wanlockhead's
economy was, for generations, driven by
lead, while gold provided temptation for
those seeking a more glamorous fortune.
Gold is still found in the burns of these
parts and you can try your hand at gold-
panning at the village's Museum of Lead
Mining. Alternatively, buy a panning
licence and, who knows, you might be as
lucky as the Canadian who recently found
a 20-carat nugget.

From the Museum of Lead Mining take
the steps at the end of the car park, cross
the road and join the waymarked
Southern Upland Way. Pass the houses
and wend your way uphill over open
moorland. This is fine walking country
at any time of year. In August it shimmers
with purple heather and you'll hear the
distinctive 'go-back, back, back' call of the
red grouse, while during the snowy
winter months it is home to the
intermediate slopes of the community-
run Lowther Hills Ski Club.

◀ Wanlockhead from the Southern Upland Way

Carry on over a wooden bridge and turn right on joining the tarmac service road. Just round the bend and at the end of the crash barrier take the grassy path off to the right, again turning right when it rejoins the service road. Continue to the large gap in the crash barrier, go right and follow your nose across the rough open moorland until it meets a track and fence. Turn right and head down to the saddle, a low point between the hills. Off to the left is the Enterkin Pass, an old travellers' route crossing the Lowther Hills to Glasgow. Daniel Defoe in *A Tour Thro' the Whole Island of Great Britain* (1726) described it as 'Enterkin, the frightfullest pass, and most dangerous that I met with, between that and Penmenmuir in North Wales'.

From here, keep the fence to your left and climb steeply to the top of East Mount Lowther (Auchenlone), which is classed as a Donald – a hill in central or southern Scotland of at least 610m (2000ft) in height with a drop of at least 30m (98ft) all round. If it isn't too windy this makes a great pitstop, offering fine views down Nithsdale to the Solway Firth and, on a clear day, the Cumbrian hills beyond.

When ready, head back down to the saddle and take the path off to the left under the pylons, crossing a burn and rejoining the tarmac service road. From here simply retrace your earlier route to Wanlockhead, where various attractions await: the Museum of Lead Mining, Lochnell mineshaft and the second oldest workers' subscription library in Europe dating from 1756; the oldest is at Leadhills just down the road.

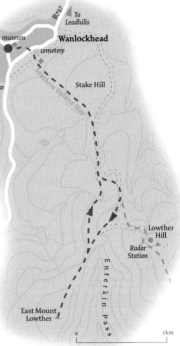

Wanlockhead to Sanquhar

Distance 13km **Time** 4 hours
Terrain footpaths and upland tracks
(detour may be in place during shooting
season) **Map** OS Explorer 329
Access parking in Sanquhar, then bus
to Wanlockhead and walk back; bus to
Sanquhar from Dumfries; train station
in Sanquhar

If tramping the entire Southern Upland
Way feels a little too energetic then this
more manageable taster might be just the
ticket. The full 340km route, usually
walked west to east, links Portpatrick on
Galloway's southwest coast to
Cockburnspath in the Scottish Borders
near the North Sea. This section flows
against that tide (not that you are likely to
see many people) in a gentle descent from
Wanlockhead with glorious views over
Nithsdale on the final drop into Sanquhar.

Start from the Museum of Lead Mining
at the heart of Wanlockhead, Scotland's

highest village, where it's well worth a
visit to swot up on man's influence on
this dramatic landscape. While it was lead
that brought the village into existence
there's also gold 'in them thar hills' and
you can still pan for it today: just
purchase a licence from the museum first.

From the museum cross the road and
follow the course of Wanlock Water out of
the village, looking for the tell-tale signs
of an industrial past – old bings, the
entrances to abandoned mines (one of
which can be visited) and Britain's only
surviving water-powered beam engine
used for pumping the water out of mines.
After about 3km cross the narrow
footbridge over the burn for the first of
the walk's two short climbs as the path
contours up the slope, offering fine views
over the Lowther Hills.

There is a short stretch of moorland at
the top, then carry on downhill aiming for
the ruined cottage at Cogshead. This

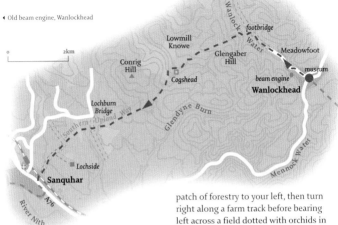

◄ Old beam engine, Wanlockhead

stands at the centre of an old Celtic burial ground – the circular graves of grassed-over heaps of stones are tricky to make out. Just after the cottage turn left to follow the main track for about 300m, then left again onto a path that initially climbs gently, followed by a steeper section that lasts for around 150m. Cresting the hill, continue straight ahead keeping to the stone dyke on your left.

Now Nithsdale begins to open up ahead, summer bringing the song of skylarks as they zip across the sky. With luck, the daytime-flying short-eared owl might also put in an appearance as it hunts for its quarry. Dropping downhill, also keep an eye open for Crawick Multiverse just to the north of Sanquhar, a mighty landscape art installation exploring the universe. Keep ahead, with a

patch of forestry to your left, then turn right along a farm track before bearing left across a field dotted with orchids in spring and summer.

Pause to take in the view over Sanquhar at Matthew's Folly, where a cairn marks the centenary celebrations of the Riding of the Marches, the annual tradition of inspecting and protecting the burgh boundaries against the warring English and other skirmishing clans. On a sunny day watch for the flutter of orange butterfly wings: small pearl-bordered fritillaries and small heaths fly hereabouts.

From here, simply continue down into Sanquhar, turning right along the historic high street, passing first the obelisk marking the 1680 pinning of the Sanquhar Declarations to the old town cross and then the world's oldest working post office, operating since 1712. The little seasonal museum in the old Tolbooth is worth a visit to see the intricate Sanquhar knitwear designs alone.

15

Drumlanrig and the Marr Burn

Distance 4km **Time** 1 hour
Terrain footpaths and woodland tracks
Map OS Explorer 321 **Access** parking at
Drumlanrig Castle (seasonal entrance
charges apply); bus from Thornhill and
Sanquhar stops on the A702 (2km walk)

**Drumlanrig Castle is one of the
region's most iconic buildings and sits
at the heart of the Duke of Buccleuch's
36,000-hectare Queensberry Estate.
This route follows the blue arrows from
the castle through glorious woodland
and past old stone bridges and Andy
Goldsworthy's Leaping Arch to a view of
the castle and gardens framed by
towering trees.**

The estate grounds offer walkers and
mountain bikers a stunning mix of woods
and parkland to explore, crisscrossed with
burns and a sprinkling of lochs. The
walking trails are easy to follow, identified
by coloured waymarkers, and range from
the short and simple to a more strenuous
climb to Mount Malloch.

Like all of the walks at Drumlanrig,
this route, described as 'A Turn Along the
Marr Burn', begins at the castle. The 'Pink
Palace' – as it is affectionately known –
was crafted from local sandstone in the
17th century for the 1st Duke of
Queensberry and simply glows on a
sunny day.

Local legend has it that the Duke only
spent a single night here after a night of
calling out for his servants who, due to
the size of the castle, failed to hear his
shouts. He promptly packed up and
headed back to the more modest
Sanquhar Castle just down the road.

From the car park follow the path uphill
through a lovely woodland of spruce,
larch, sycamore and beech. Along the way
the path is bisected by mountain bike

◄ Leaping Arch

trails, so keep an eye out for approaching cyclists. Ford the small burn and continue downhill, passing an old stone bridge before turning right alongside pretty Druid Loch, home to kingfisher and otter.

Nip across the estate road and bridge over the waters of Marr Burn, continuing uphill before dropping back down to follow the burnside path. Cross the stone bridge and follow the burn to the Leaping Arch, designed and constructed by internationally renowned local artist Andy Goldsworthy. Commissioned by the 10th Duke of Buccleuch and 12th Duke of Queensberry, the installation represents a salmon leaping upstream and makes a perfect spot to sit and enjoy the peace and tranquillity.

Cross the bridge and head uphill along the woodland path. The trees begin to thin, offering glimpses of the formal gardens before revealing a stunning view of the castle.

Once back down at the waterside, look out for dippers along the man-made Cascade. This watery feature was created by the 3rd Duke of Queensberry and was a logistical headache from the outset, but today it burbles away and is simply left to the forces of nature. Cross the burn and follow the path alongside the ha-ha – a ditch and wall that creates a boundary without disturbing the view – and open parkland, passing a magnificent 300-year-old sycamore, Britain's largest, before returning to the castle car park.

Durisdeer Well Path

Distance 6.5km Time 2 hours
Terrain tracks and hill paths (sometimes
muddy and boggy) Map OS Explorer 329
Access park considerately by the church;
no public transport to the start

Starting from the tiny, picture perfect
village of Durisdeer, with its handful of
pretty cottages and fine church, this walk
follows in the footsteps of Romans and
pilgrims through a glen framed by the
beautifully-sculpted Lowther Hills.

The village sits at the end of a narrow
dead-end road, a spot easily overlooked by
today's travellers, but this wasn't always
the case. It might come as a surprise that
the Romans ventured further north than
Hadrian's Wall, building this main route
from Nithsdale up into Clydesdale and
creating fortifications as they went. Later,
more pious footsteps passed this way as
pilgrims, including James IV, undertook
the 250km trek from Edinburgh to
Whithorn Priory in Galloway. Nowadays
the A702, through the Dalveen Pass,

carries traffic well away from the village,
leaving those who venture here and up
onto the moors with a calming peace
and isolation.

From the church take the road off to
the right and through the metal gate onto
the southern slopes of the Lowther Hills.
Keeping to the main track along the
drystane dyke, after about 1km follow the
fingerpost guiding you half-left across the
grassland, over the Kirk Burn and on to
the Roman fortlet, considered one of the
best preserved in the region. Measuring
roughly 31m by 18m, it was built during
the 2nd century Antonine period as one

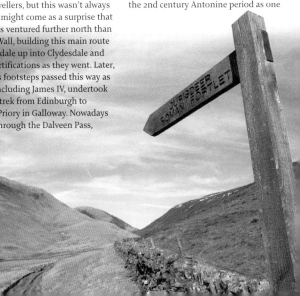

of a series set about 16km apart to house detachments from the main forts and to stamp Roman authority on the local population. Today it is a lovely spot to sit and enjoy the views all around, with few signs of modern-day man.

Continue along the glen, following the track past the fortlet and soon reaching a rusting tin hut, full of nesting swallows during the summer months. The hut makes for a surprisingly good photo opportunity, contrasting with scree and heather-clad slopes all around. The next few hundred metres are a bit harder and damper underfoot; the track becomes less distinct, often little more than a sheep run in places and increasingly boggy. Head for the drystane dyke climbing up to the col, so follow your nose a bit and seek the route of least bogginess.

At the top take a well-earned rest and feast your eyes on the fine view back down the glen into Nithsdale and on to the Galloway hills beyond. Go through the gate and turn right to follow the broad clear track back down to Durisdeer. Before doing so, though, nip left to the next gate for yet another lovely view down into the next valley.

On the return leg to Durisdeer the outgoing route is laid out before you, including a great view of the fortlet, the size and structure of which can now be clearly discerned. Once back in the village change out of your muddy boots and be sure to visit the kirk, a building notably out of proportion for the number of residents and of a style quite unlike other Scottish churches.

The reason lies with the nearby Drumlanrig Castle and estate, seat of the Dukes of Queensberry, who used this as their parish kirk. The extravagant mausoleum, built by the 1st Duke of Queensberry, is located at the rear and houses the fabulous Queensberry Marbles, an elaborate memorial to the 2nd Duke of Queensberry and his wife Mary, which should not be missed.

◀ On the Well Path

19

Morton Loch and Castle

Distance 8.5km **Time** 2 hours 30
Terrain footpaths, farm fields, tracks and
quiet roads (cattle at Morton Mains)
Map OS Explorer 329 or 321 **Access** parking
in the old quarry just under the railway
bridge east of Carronbridge; buses from
Dumfries stop in Carronbridge (1km)

From the remains of an old quarry on the
edge of Carronbridge, just north of the
attractive town of Thornhill, this route
wends its way through Morton Wood
plantation to the atmospheric ruins of
Morton Castle.

The walk begins and ends by wriggling
along forestry trails, offering fine views
along Nithsdale. Stately Drumlanrig
Castle nestles in the valley below the
heather-clad peaks of the southern
Lowther Hills. Along the way Morton
Castle is arguably the area's most
enigmatic, debated and remote ruin and

one of only a few surviving hall-houses.

From the parking area take the forestry
track uphill into the woods and stay on
this main track for around 2km as it
zigzags through the plantation. The track
soon curves left onto a straight stretch
offering the first views of Nithsdale. Stay
on the main track through a quick
succession of turns – left, right and right
again – to climb uphill and then sweep
around to the right. At the top of the
steeper section ignore the waymarked
track off to the left (which is the return
route), continuing instead ahead, around
the open grassland, looking towards
Thornhill and the hills beyond. This
section of plantation is softened with
fringes of beech and birch, while the tracks
are lined with fungi, heather and mosses.

The track heads back into the woods,
curving left at the waymarker post
looking towards the wonderfully named

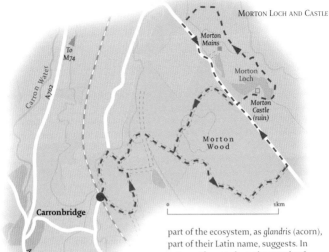

To M74

A702

Carron Water

Morton Mains

Morton Loch

Morton Castle (ruin)

Morton Wood

Carronbridge

A76

To Thornhill

0   1km

part of the ecosystem, as *glandris* (acorn), part of their Latin name, suggests. In autumn they can bury thousands of acorns, many of which will be forgotten. 'Mighty oaks from little acorns grow', as the saying goes.

Take the grassy path uphill, which is ever more overgrown as it curves around to follow the fenceline. Go left at the track and, following the fingerposts, continue above the farm and cross the field with the woodland pasture information board. (To avoid any curious cattle, either nip higher up the hill or drop down into the lower field.) At the end of the field, turn left along the hawthorn hedge and head down to join the road.

Go left up the road back to the castle entrance and then turn right onto the plantation track. Follow the waymarker arrows through the wood, soon rejoining the outbound route to drop down the hill. When the track forks go right and, at the road, turn left to return to the start.

Bellybought Hill. Turn left along the tarmac road bounded with gnarled trees, and soon the distinctive ruin of Morton Castle comes into view. Perched atop a pretty man-made loch, the castle is thought to be late 13th century with connections to both the Douglases and Maxwells. This is a lovely spot for a romantic picnic and many older locals still talk fondly of their days wooing and courting here.

Having explored the castle's nooks and crannies, take the Morton Heritage & Nature Trail down to the right and around the end of the loch. Pass through the gate into a native woodland full of ancient oaks, looking out for the resident jays. These enigmatic birds are an important

Queensberry Hills

Distance 11.5km **Time** 4 hours 30
Terrain tracks and pathless rough hillside
Map OS Explorer 321 **Access** one parking
place on the verge by the footpath sign;
no public transport to the start

If Dumfries is the Queen of the South,
then Queensberry must arguably be
Queen of the Dales, with Wee
Queensberry its princess. This prominent
Dumfriesshire landmark stands proud at
the southern reaches of the Lowther Hills
and offers some challenging yet
rewarding upland walking. These are
lonely moorland hills, swaddled in
heather, sprinkled with rocky outcrops
and brimming with wildlife.

The scenery, stunning in grandeur, is
crisscrossed by few paths and even fewer
prominent features, making precise
directions difficult, although the odd
cairn helps guide the way. The lumpy,
steep hillsides make for slow progress,

but each hard-earned step is rewarded
with increasingly glorious views. It's
unlikely you will come across anyone else;
even the sheep look slightly taken aback
to see you. On a clear day this is
magnificent walking country, but in
poor visibility it can be treacherous; be
prepared with map, compass and the
skills to use them.

Start from the roadside pull-in with the
footpath sign close to Mitchellslacks
Farm, 10km north of Ae. Drop down to the
track over the Capel Water and go left past
Mitchellslacks Farm, looking out for
graceful fork-tailed red kites. Go through
two metal gates and then gently uphill on
the stony track, leaving the drystane dyke.
After about 1km take the track to the
right, running around The Law, and soon
drop down to some stone sheep fanks. Go
through the gate, past the fanks, and
carefully ford the burn (tricky after rain)
to follow the track uphill.

◀ Cairn on the side of Queensberry

When this abruptly ends, stay with the faint uphill path. After a while it starts to curve right, heading away from the cairn above High Church. At this point turn left to ascend the hillside. There isn't a path – simply pick the route of least struggle to the cairn. If you accidentally arrive above a deep gully, skirt left around this to get back on track.

At the cairn turn left, crossing the heather-covered flatness of Craih Hill, then take a broad right-curving arc aiming for a climb up the left flank of Wee Queensberry, which avoids the gullies on the more direct route. Pick up the faint path at the base of Wee Queensberry, climb steeply up around the scree slope and go for the final push to the trig point at the top.

Continue ahead to the next cairn, then drop down to the start of the demanding hike up Queensberry Hill. A spot of wildlife watching may offer up the perfect excuse to stop along the way: ravens caw, skylark sing and mountain hare dash about the hillside (still with their white coats well into spring).

For a less steep ascent initially keep over to the right side of the hill and, after the indistinct burns, start to curve left up towards the distant cairn. This disappears from view, but keep going and it will eventually reappear. Once you reach it, turn right for the final climb to the massive summit cairn and spectacular views across Dumfriesshire and beyond.

Retrace the route to the previous cairn, then continue diagonally right down off the hill. The descent soon joins a faint track, which becomes more pronounced; follow this all the way down to a main track in the valley bottom by Capel Burn.

Turn left along the track, noting the atmospheric cottage ruins off to the right, which must have been a harsh place to live, and follow it all the way back to the start.

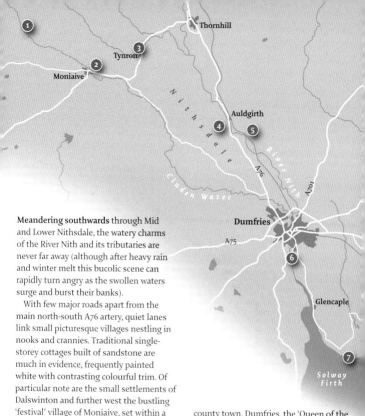

Meandering southwards through Mid and Lower Nithsdale, the watery charms of the River Nith and its tributaries are never far away (although after heavy rain and winter melt this bucolic scene can rapidly turn angry as the swollen waters surge and burst their banks).

With few major roads apart from the main north-south A76 artery, quiet lanes link small picturesque villages nestling in nooks and crannies. Traditional single-storey cottages built of sandstone are much in evidence, frequently painted white with contrasting colourful trim. Of particular note are the small settlements of Dalswinton and further west the bustling 'festival' village of Moniaive, set within a more rugged landscape at the meeting point of three steep-sided glens.

Scotland's national poet, Robert Burns, moved to Nithsdale from Ayrshire to farm at Ellisland, where the romantic setting inspired some of his most famous works (albeit while exposing his considerable lack of flair for farming). Further down the dale on the banks of the Nith lies the county town, Dumfries, the 'Queen of the South', while further still the undulations finally give way to the mudflats and merse of the Nith estuary as it flows onwards to the Solway Firth. This tidal bounty feeds thousands of wading birds, attracting massive winter migrations of geese and whooper swans with their old-fashioned honking car horn call, arriving from colder climes around the Arctic Circle.

Caerlaverock Castle ▶

Mid and Lower Nithsdale

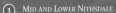

Striding Arches

Distance 10km **Time** 3 hours
Terrain forest hardcore road and open
hillside **Map** OS Explorer 328
Access parking area at Cairnhead before
metal barrier; buses from Thornhill and
Dumfries to Moniaive, but no public
transport for the final 11km to the start
– hitchhiking has some success

Heading out of Moniaive, the isolated
and dramatic valley of the Dalwhat Water
soon envelops the senses. A car to the
start is really the only option, unless the
340km Southern Upland Way is your
approach route!

The single-track road to the start gives
way to a rough forestry road and it's easy
to wonder if you've taken a wrong turn,
but keep going and a small parking area
with information boards is eventually
reached. If the metal barrier is open don't
drive beyond it as you may find it locked
on your return. It would be a lonely night

on the hill, albeit with some of the best
star gazing in the country.

The first of Andy Goldsworthy's striking
art installations is close at hand, tucked
away just above the parking area at the
old byre of Cairnhead steading. This is an
effective introduction to the Striding
Arches that adorn the three surrounding
peaks (this walk goes only to one other).
Despite being 4m high with a span of 7m
and constructed from 31 local red
sandstone blocks weighing in at some 27
tons, the arches are surprisingly well
blended into the landscape.

Around the byre also keep an eye open
for various stone carvings, including the
old names for Cairnhead – *Conraicht* (1547),
Bonrick (1600), *Conrig* (1804) – and the roll
call of shepherds that once called this
lonely spot home.

Return to the parking area and then
follow the forestry track past the metal
barrier and on up into the valley. This is a

◄ Striding Arch at Colt Hill

very straightforward walk: just stay on the main forestry access track for 4km, passing numerous tumbling burns, crossing a wooden bridge and ignoring the forest road that goes off to the left. Gradually climbing ever deeper into the forested hills, try to imagine how the landscape of yesteryear looked. This was once all sheep country, home to six farming settlements, or fermtouns, but as times became harder the shepherd's place in this lonely glen was replaced by today's more profitable crop of conifers.

Continue on the track as it swings sharply right to rise more steeply for about 1.5km, on through a metal gate and around a kink in the road, arriving at a wooden fingerpost. Now it's time to leave the forest road by turning right and climbing another hill, keeping to the left of the fence up the open hillside for 500m to the top of Colt Hill and the pinnacle of its own Striding Arch.

A crucial factor in Andy Goldsworthy choosing the three peaks of Colt Hill, Benbrack and Bail Hill was that the arches had to be linked by open sightlines. On a clear day, this is a place to revel in the commanding view.

Stop a while; pause, reflect and enjoy the isolation and solitude, and, once fully rejuvenated, retrace each step for the 4.5km return journey back down to the start point.

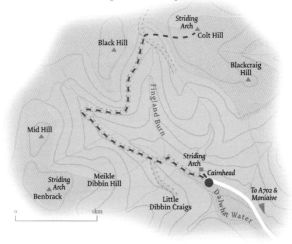

Moniaive and Bardennoch Hill

Distance 7.5km **Time** 2 hours 30
Terrain tracks, open hillside (carefully
over a couple of dykes) and quiet roads
Maps OS Explorer 320/321 & 328 **Access** car
park in village at bottom of Dunreggan
Brae; buses from Dumfries and Thornhill

Moniaive is oft hailed as one of Britain's
'coolest' and 'most buzzing' villages
thanks to a full programme of events
throughout the year, and for such a
sparsely populated area it certainly packs
plenty of creative punch. Originally
famed for artists such as James Paterson
and E A Hornel of the Glasgow Boys
movement, it was later home to *Black
Narcissus* author, Rumer Godden, and
more recently Alex Kapranos of funk
rockers Franz Ferdinand.

From the car park, turn right and then
right again to cross the old stone bridge
with a first glimpse of the historic High
Street, lined with coaching inns, an
inviting café and a sprinkling of shops.
Continue past the Market Cross and, at
the Clock House, built as the
schoolmaster's house in 1865, turn right
up North Street with its pretty painted
cottages and unusual parish church.

Just after Hastings Hall turn right,
signed Bardennoch, and then climb
uphill along the edge of a wood to emerge
onto open hillside. Continue along the
track lined with drystane dykes and up
past the atmospheric ruins of Upper
Bardennoch farm.

As the track peters out stay with the
dyke up through the stand of firs and over
the top of Bardennoch Hill, pausing a
while to enjoy the views. Continue
straight ahead to the gate in the dyke that
runs in front of the wood – nip through
this to visit the pretty lochan; otherwise
stay on this side, turning right and
keeping the dyke and wood on your left.

Cross a tumbled dyke and carefully over the mesh fence, before heading across the next field and through the gate a little uphill, halfway along the fenceline. Go straight over the next field and at the tall drystane dyke follow it to the right. Passing through a gate, turn immediately left and carry on through another gate.

Turning right, wander around the hill and, once through the next gate, turn right along the road known as Dunreggan Brae. Follow this all the way back to Moniaive, with fine views of the glens at every step.

Once back in the village turn left by the bridge and follow the street out to the edge of the once-separate village of Dunreggan. Just after the bowls club turn right down past the playing field and on to the John Corrie Wildlife Garden, created in honour of a local Edwardian historian and naturalist. This attractive spot is packed with wildflowers and feeders aflutter with birds, plus the intriguing Moniaive Geodial created from rocks and fossils from around the county.

Cross the bridge and head left along the raised path as it meanders along the Waters of Dalwhat, Cairn and Craigdarroch, looping back round to Moniaive. At the farm go through the metal gate and turn right along the road back into the village, but be sure to take a detour down the side of the school to visit the old railway station. Once back at the Market Cross, turn right and return along the High Street to the start.

◄ Looking up Bardennoch Hill

Auchengibbert Hill and Tynron Doon

Distance **6.5km** Time **3 hours**
Terrain **forestry tracks and open hills**
Map **OS Explorer 321** Access **parking at
the village hall; buses from Thornhill
and Moniaive**

The picture-perfect village of Tynron
offers a most cordial introduction to this
taxing upland walk, albeit one of
exquisite views, peace and sanctuary.
Once out on the open hills the knee-
jarring steep sections, boggy bits and
lack of paths can make for hard work, but
don't be put off as this route is up there
with the finest in the Dumfriesshire
Dales. So, limber up and set off in the
footsteps of our Iron Age ancestors.

From the village hall go left and
immediately left again along a road of
painted cottages overlooked by the
deconsecrated kirk perched on the

prominent knoll. The road soon becomes
a track rising up into the woods and
curves sharply right before offering a
choice of paths – take the left-hand fork
uphill (the right-hand waymarked track is
the return route).

Carry on past a couple of delightfully
situated cottages, following the track
around to the left and through the gate.
Continue through the next gate and here
leave the comfort of the track to walk
diagonally right uphill. After 300m pass
through the gate just to the left of a
sheep fank, turn immediately left and go
through another gate, then climb steeply
uphill, initially following the rylock mesh
fence, then over open hill. If visibility is
fine, you are aiming for the distant gate in
the fenceline just before the hill summit;
otherwise be sure to use a map and
compass to check the direction. For much

of this section it will be just you, a few hundred sheep, the gruff caw of raven and towering song of skylark.

Go through the gate and diagonally left for the final push to the top of Auchengibbert Hill, crowned with an old OS triangulation pillar. Over the last 1km you will have gained some 200m in height, but there is no shame in a breather along the way to enjoy the fine views up Shinnel Glen and, once at the top, around all points of the compass.

Leave the hill in an easterly direction (roughly the way you came), picking up a faint path that soon crosses a tumbled drystane dyke. Continue straight ahead to follow the line of another toppled dyke, staying with it as it bends half-right.

It's time to leave the dyke when it turns sharp right; from here follow your nose over the open hill across the top of Mid Hill, down to the col at Crystal Knowes, then steeply up to the summit of the distinctively shaped Tynron Doon. Note that any sign of a path dips in and out along the way. The mighty 'Doon' was

worked by Iron Age man creating its distinctive tiered defensive hilltop position and you certainly feel on top of the world up here.

Take a turn around the top to spot the more obvious downhill path (on the southwest side). It soon disappears but keep contouring the hillside, nipping over a few small burns along the way. The whole time keep heading for the gate just before and to the right of the precipitous wood on Craigturra. Go through the gate, ford the Craigturra Burn and continue through another gate onto a track that soon enters the conifer woods. On leaving the trees follow the track back to Tynron village.

◀ Tynron Doon's hillfort summit

Glenmidge and Lag Tower

Distance 7.5km **Time** 2 hours 30
Terrain tracks, upland fields and quiet
roads **Map** OS Explorer 321 **Access** limited
parking at roadside; essentially no public
transport to the start – just a single
fortnightly bus from Dumfries/Thornhill,
although frequent buses from the same
towns stop at Auldgirth (3km walk)

The tiny clachan of Glenmidge nestles
serenely at the head of an almost hidden
Nithsdale valley in a landscape with a
hint of J R R Tolkien's Middle Earth: lush
green lumps and bumps sprinkled with
moss-coated woodlands. Whitewashed
farm steadings pepper the hillsides, each
framed by a matrix of drystane dykes.
Throw into this delightful mix an
atmospheric ruin or two and you've got
the recipe for a most seductive ramble.

From the roadside follow the core path
(Lag Tower) sign and climb uphill along a
broad track through a woodland alive
with birdsong. At the wood edge continue

along the track as it veers right. Initially
crossing open hillside, it soon takes on
the feel of an old drovers' route edged
with drystane dykes.

Head left past the now ruined Upper
Hallidayhill, which once must have been a
sizeable but exposed farmhouse and
outbuildings, with fine views north to the
Lowther Hills. Carry on along the wiggling
track for about 1km, then go through the
wooden gate on the right into the conifer
woods and drop steeply downhill. At the
bottom go through another gate and stay
with the track following the drystane
dyke, soon popping out at a road just to
the side of Lag Tower ruins.

The tower has a long and proud history,
being the historical seat of the Grierson
Clan – in fact, if you are a Greer, Grier or
Grierson it's likely you can trace your
family history back to the Dumfriesshire
Griersons. The tower's exact age is a little
foggy; however, the clan's historical jigsaw
indicates a probable founding date of

◄ Farm track near Glenmidge

around 1439. The last resident, Sir Robert Grierson, 1st Baronet of Lag, was also the best known, and most feared. To many in the area he was 'Auld' or 'Cruel' Lag, an enthusiastic and inventive persecutor of rebellious Covenanters during 'The Killing Time' of the late 17th century; according to local legend he is said to have rolled captured rebels down a nearby hillside in spiked barrels!

If you fancy extending the route, you can easily tag on a loop at this point by turning left at the road by Lag Tower. From here take the track opposite Blacksteps, go past Dempsterton Farm to the road, turn left and then left again, passing Swyre and returning to Lag Tower.

To keep going without the additional loop, turn right along the quiet road and, after about 500m, go left onto an even quieter road that meanders along past Low Kirkbride and Kirkbride farms. Just after the latter turn right onto a broad track framed on each side by a drystane

dyke. Immediately after the cottage ruins turn right along an uphill track leading around the north side of Kirkbride Hill.

At the end of the track wrestle your way through or over the gate arrangement and keep ahead along the dyke, crossing over or through another gate and then rejoining the track. Continue downhill along the tarmac, enjoying the fine Nithsdale views.

At the road turn right and then, after about 300m, right again, heading downhill and through Glenmidge in the bottom of the valley. Cross the Glenmidge Burn, pass the old mill and carry on straight ahead to return to the start.

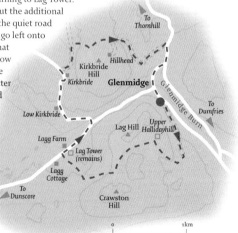

Dalswinton tour

Distance 5.5km **Time** 2 hours
Terrain woodland footpath and quiet
roads **Map** OS Explorer 321 **Access** parking
in a wide road entrance between Duncow
and Dalswinton just before the entrance
gates to Dalswinton estate; buses from
Dumfries and Thornhill

The estate surrounding Dalswinton House
is a beautifully kept secret. Until 1355 a
castle almost certainly sat on the mound
occupied by the 18th-century house built
by Patrick Miller, who bought the estate in
1785. He also created the artificial loch at
the centre of this gentle circular walk, on
which he launched the world's first
steamboat in 1788. Today Dalswinton
remains privately owned, the family home
of the Landale family since 1919.

From the parking spot, turn right along
the road towards Auldgirth and enter the
estate grounds on the left through the
gates between two lodge houses. Follow
the drive, bearing left where a road joins
from the right, with a view to the left of a
ruined tower, all that remains of an earlier
laird's house. At the gates leading to the
house itself, take the road to the right
along the edge of Dalswinton Loch,
ornamented with boathouse and, at the
far end, a round doocot on an island
reached by an oriental bridge. Swans,
oystercatchers and Canada geese are
regular visitors.

Continue ahead, passing Dalswinton
Mains stables on the right, and follow the
road around to the right as an imposing
red iron railway bridge comes into view
over to the left. Where the road meets two

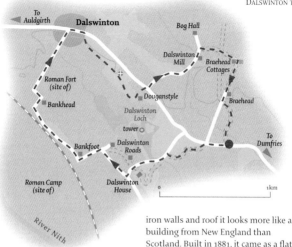

tracks from the right, follow it round to the left to pass in front of the white cottages at Bankfoot.

Keep to the road as it almost converges with the railway line and then follow it uphill with views of the Nithsdale hills opening up. Pass through Bankhead farmyard and carry on to Dalswinton village, with a view back down to Dalswinton Loch and House. On the other side of the Nith is Ellisland, the one-time home of Robert Burns, tenant and friend of Dalswinton's owner, Patrick Miller.

The road emerges at the village bus stop. Go right, passing the gaily coloured cottages and, just beyond the last one, go through a gate on the right to follow a woodland path which runs parallel to the road for around 500m. Along the way pass the striking Dalswinton Barony Church; with its bellcote, spire and red corrugated-

iron walls and roof it looks more like a building from New England than Scotland. Built in 1881, it came as a flat-pack ordered from a catalogue!

At a cross-path junction with a gate into a field on the right, cut up to the left through Douganstyle to the main road. Turn right along the road and then immediately left, signposted Maryfield, to climb for around 500m, enjoying views of Criffel in the distance to the right. Just after Dalswinton Mill – private, but with waterwheel still in situ – turn right. Where the road splits again and rises more steeply to the left take the track to the right, signposted Braehead Cottages. This leads down between the cottages to the right, with expansive views of Criffel, Dumfries and the hills beyond.

Where the track joins the road continue straight on downhill, keeping Braehead Farmhouse to the left. Shortly after, go left across a cattle grid and through a gate to follow the track back down to the start.

◀ Dalswinton Barony Church

35

Dumfries and Kingholm Quay

Distance 7km (not including town trail)
Time 2 hours **Terrain** pavement and parks
Map OS Explorer 313 **Access** parking
along the riverside at Whitesands

Combine the maritime and mercantile past of historic Dumfries with a stroll through the grounds of a pioneering former 'lunatic' asylum.

The River Nith's importance is never more apparent than in Dumfries. Waterpower and access to the Solway Firth were central to the town's past riches. For centuries its thriving port traded across the globe with the British colonies and drove the riverside mills. At one time, so much tobacco, coal, lime, brandy and wine also came ashore here that Dumfries became known as 'Scotland's Liverpool'.

Starting from Whitesands cross the 17th-century Devorgilla's 'Old' Bridge spanning the River Nith. Turn left along the riverbank before re-crossing at the

Suspension Bridge, built in 1875 to help the mostly female mill workers – some 1200 a day – get to work.

Turn right and cross the busy road into Dock Park, a classic Victorian town park complete with café, bowling green and bandstand, plus views over to the old Rosefield Mill. Look out for the *Titanic* memorial, dedicated to two local men lost in April 1912. One of them, John Law Hume, was a violinist in the ship's band which famously played as it sank.

Continue through the park and along the tarmac riverside path heading all the way out of town to the small harbour village of Kingholm Quay. Originally part of the town port, today it is a pleasing spot with a popular pub. Turning right at the road, pass the harbourside buildings and follow the road sharp left uphill.

At the roundabout go left, cross the road and go through Brownhall Gate into the grounds of The Crichton.

◄ Kingholm Quay

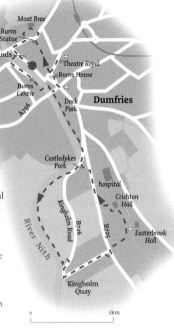

Left a considerable sum of money on her husband's death in 1823, Elizabeth Crichton set about trying to create Scotland's fifth university, but resistance from its rivals led her to form The Crichton Institution for Lunatics, described as 'the best in Europe', instead. It became known for its moral approach to mental health and pioneered early forms of occupational and art therapy. Today The Crichton offers the educational dream of its founder, serving as a remote campus for numerous universities.

At the T-junction turn left and veer diagonally right up to the Crichton Memorial Church, built in 1897. From the entrance, continue off to the left across the grass, follow the long low building before going left, then right at its end. In front of Crichton Hall go left and drop down into the landscaped grounds with its waterfalls and rock gardens. Follow the network of paths off to the right, down to the gate at the main road.

Crossing the road, turn right and after about 250m enter Castledykes Park, the site of Dumfries Castle. Follow the path down through the park (taking a detour left to the Sunken Garden, with its carving of Robert the Bruce) and at the bottom gate cross the road to rejoin the outbound route.

To also explore the town centre's key sights, turn right out of Dock Park and up to St Michael's Kirk (Burns Mausoleum),

cross the busy road and carry on down Burns Street for Burns' House, turning right at the end of Burns Street to the Theatre Royal (one of Scotland's oldest) or left for the High Street and a few of Burns' favourite watering holes like The Globe. At the Burns statue go right, then left down Irving Street for Moat Brae, where J M Barrie invented Peter Pan's Neverland. To return to the start head down Buccleuch Street (the main A780) back to Whitesands.

Caerlaverock and Ward Law

Distance 8km **Time** 2 hours 30
Terrain footpath, boardwalk and quiet
roads **Map** OS Explorer 322 **Access** parking
at Castle Corner car park on the B725,
bus from Dumfries

A meander around Caerlaverock on the
Solway Firth south of Dumfries takes in
picturesque castle ruins, the remains of
an Iron Age fort, miles of wetlands and
year-round wildlife highlights. Covering
almost 20,000 acres, Caerlaverock
National Nature Reserve is a vast flat
expanse of sand, mud, sea and merse
stretching some 16km. The unusual
name is derived from the old Scots for a
skylark – *a laverock* – thus Caerlaverock is
either 'Castle of the Lark' or 'Lark's Nest'
and each year more than 300 pairs fill the
sky here with their towering song.

This is a truly special environment for
wildlife enthusiasts as the firth remains
in a largely natural state, creating for the
thousands of migrating birds that return

year after year a huge natural larder.
This is also a haven for rare and bizarre
creatures, including the eerie chorus of
dune-dwelling natterjack toads and
obscure tadpole shrimp, one of the
world's oldest creatures.

Before leaving Castle Corner, enjoy the
glorious views across the merse and Nith
estuary to dramatic Criffel standing at
570m, the highest peak on this coastal
fringe. Follow the footpath in amongst
the gnarled oaks of Castle Wood, skirting
the edge of the merse, which is dotted
with flowers in season: purple loosestrife,
meadowsweet and birdsfoot trefoil (or,
more evocatively, Granny's Toenails).
If here in summer, also look out for the
beautiful Scotch Argus butterfly.

Continue on the path ahead through
the woods rather than taking any paths
off to the right, which are part of the
return route. The path becomes a track by
a couple of cottages, soon opening up on
the left with an impressive view of

◀ Ward Law from Caerlaverock

Caerlaverock Castle across the reeds. The 13th-century red-pink sandstone castle is well worth the entrance fee, with moat, bridge, towers to climb and corners to explore. It's an unusual shape, three-sided, for it's believed to be built on a triangular piece of rock.

Leave the castle by the main gate and, at the junction with the road, go straight over and follow the footpath up Ward Law. It might only stand at 95m but with few high points on the estuary, it provides expansive views over the Solway Firth. Pass around the right side of the hill, taking the footpath to descend through a field and down to the road. Go straight across and follow a small road down to the Wetlands & Wildfowl Trust (WWT) Caerlaverock (3km), with its information centre, tearoom and nature reserve.

Entrance to the reserve is free for WWT members and, time permitting, worth paying if not. It's an international place – in summer the Senegalese flag flies to welcome back the migrating ospreys, while in winter it's the Icelandic flag, for it is to Caerlaverock each year that some 300 honking whooper swans return. Also, the entire Svalbard population – all 35,000-plus – of barnacle geese returns to the Solway Firth each year. From WWT, take the often-boggy track to the right immediately before the entrance to the centre and then continue through a gate on the right. The path runs between two fences across fields before reaching the Flooders boardwalk through the reeds.

Keep following the boardwalk along the merse and, on re-entering Castle Wood, turn left to soon rejoin the woodland path. Follow this back to the car park at Castle Corner.

The River Annan rises at the head of Annandale, flowing south along the length of the valley down to the Solway Firth. In these same hills, two bigger rivers also rise: the Tweed, which wends its way eastwards to the North Sea, and the Clyde, running north to Glasgow. For hillwalkers, this is the place to be. Moffat, the unofficial 'capital' of Upper Annandale, bills itself as the 'Heart of Southern Scotland' and, while you can no longer bathe in its 'health-giving' spa waters as our Victorian predecessors did, it remains a very pleasant town. Be sure to find time to browse its fine streets and independent shops before donning your boots to explore the quiet hills and glens of the surrounding Southern Uplands.

The area is home to the highest hills in Dumfriesshire, with names such as White Coomb and Hart Fell tempting walkers onwards. It's easy to escape here and not see another soul all day, with just sheep, feral goats and swirling upland birds for company. And although virtually impossible to see, this is also the home of Britain's rarest freshwater fish and relic of the Ice Age, the vendace, which is found in lonely Loch Skeen above the Grey Mare's Tail waterfall.

For more intrepid walkers the 340km Southern Upland Way passes west to east and the Annandale Way wiggles south for 88km to the Solway. Upper Annandale walking isn't all about strenuous climbs, however, and included here are a few flatter routes that are not without interest of their own.

Authors and poets such as Robert Burns, Sir Walter Scott and the Ettrick Shepherd, James Hogg, have all been inspired by the area. Despite its beauty, it remains something of a hidden gem and is always a treat to explore.

Loch Skeen ▶

Upper Annandale

The Devil's Beeftub

Distance 10km **Time** 3 hours
Terrain footpaths, open hills, grazing
fields **Map** OS Explorer 330 **Access** parking
in lay-by on A701 at Beeftub viewpoint;
no public transport to the start

The view from the roadside is certainly
impressive, but relatively few visitors
venture far from the parking area
overlooking the cavernous hollow of the
Devil's Beeftub. If they do explore the
upper reaches of the Annan Water valley
they'll discover a tranquil landscape
which once formed part of an ancient
forest now being slowly regenerated
by the Borders Forest Trust.

The Beeftub has to be one of the
Southern Uplands' most impressive
natural features and it's easy to see why it
was once used for hiding stolen cattle.
The local Johnstone clan is far more
respectable these days, but in the 16th
century they were notorious night-riding
cross-border raiders known as 'devils' to
those they plundered. The beeftub was
also jokingly known as the 'Marquis of
Annandale's Beef-stand.'

From the parking lay-by continue along
the road verge to reach the forestry track,
go through the metal gate and join the
uphill footpath signed Annandale Way.
A bench at the top of Annanhead Hill is
worth a pause, affording fine views down
the Annan valley and, on a clear day, as
far as the Solway Firth.

The route along the ridges and hilltops
of this higher section is clearly
waymarked with Annandale Way discs.
Follow the fenceline and drystane dyke,
crossing numerous burns and over
undulating hilltops (with some steep
sections). The views are ever-changing,
revealing all this area has to offer: upland
moor, patches of forestry, wind turbines,
craggy gorges and lush valley floor. After a
couple of kilometres pass through a metal

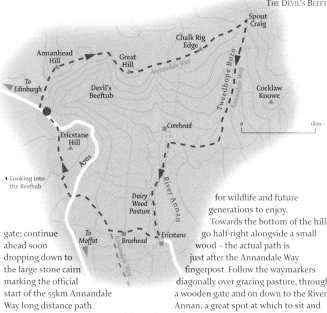

Spout Craig

Chalk Rig Edge

Annanhead Hill

Great Hill

Annandale Way

Tweedhope Burn

Annandale Way

To Edinburgh

Devil's Beeftub

Cocklaw Knowe

0   1km

Corehead

Ericstane Hill

A701

◀ Looking into the Beeftub

River Annan

Dairy Wood Pasture

for wildlife and future generations to enjoy.

gate; continue ahead soon dropping down to the large stone cairn marking the official start of the 55km Annandale Way long distance path.

To Moffat

Annandale Way

Braehead

Ericstane

Towards the bottom of the hill go half-right alongside a small wood – the actual path is just after the Annandale Way fingerpost. Follow the waymarkers diagonally over grazing pasture, through a wooden gate and on down to the River Annan, a great spot at which to sit and enjoy the valley vista and delightful bobbing of the resident dippers. Follow the farm track left, over the river and on past Dairy Wood Pasture, full of gnarly old birch and oaks, providing shade for generations of livestock.

From this stone marker turn right and head down the hill, following the route of the Tweedhope Burn. The path soon becomes a well-formed track contouring its way down to the bottom of the Annandale valley. Corehead Farm and the surrounding hills are owned and managed by the Borders Forest Trust – a 640ha site which is an interesting mix of working farm and upland woodland. This area was once cloaked in a thick mix of oak, ash, aspen, juniper, rowan, alder, willow, birch and cherry trees, part of the now much depleted Ettrick Forest. The planting of more than 230,000 trees is creating a new native woodland

Look right as you walk into Ericstane Farm and take the signed track uphill. Pass the cottage and at a T-junction of tracks turn right, climbing back up to the A701. Along the way look out for lapwing and curlew, as well as stopping to enjoy the panorama. Cross the main road carefully and follow the track up over Ericstane Hill before dropping back down to the start point above the Beeftub.

Hart Fell

Distance **13km** Time **5 hours**
Terrain **hill tracks, rough moorland and
grassy pasture** Map **OS Explorer 330**
Access **parking at the Annan Water Hall;
no public transport to the start**

Hart Fell is one of Dumfriesshire's loftiest
hills and rewards the effort to climb it
with stunning views. Isolation has long
been one of its characteristics and some
say Merlin, the wizard of Arthurian
legend, sought refuge here. In winter or
poor visibility good map-reading and
compass skills are essential for safely
completing this strenuous route.

It is said that during the late 6th
century, following his clan's defeat in
battle, Merlin lived as a hermit in the
dense forest that once cloaked Hart Fell's
flanks. Today the trees are gone and these

hills are clad in thick grass, heather
and mosses, but are no less beautiful
for that.

Start from the corrugated-iron clad
Annan Water community hall, 6km from
Moffat on the dead-end Old Edinburgh
Road. Carry on up the single-track road for
about 500m, then turn right opposite
Newton farmhouse along the track signed
Old Newton. Don't cross the burn but
instead follow the waymarker arrows
ahead and then right and left through
the farmyard and numerous gates. And
don't be surprised if the resident deer
start to follow you!

Once out on the open hillside the clear
track initially wiggles gently uphill,
gradually getting steeper. At the deer
fencing go over the large stile and follow
the faint uphill grassy track on past the

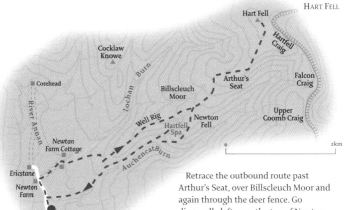

sheep fank and up along Well Rig ridge.
From early spring onwards, these hills are
alive with melodious skylarks plus the
odd chuntering from disturbed black
grouse. Look around at the views to the
Devil's Beeftub at Annandale's head and
stretching the other way down to Criffel
standing guard over the Solway Firth. Off
to the right is the craggy cleft created by
Spa Well Burn, a stop-off point further on.

Go through the deer fence and follow
the path up to Billscleuch Moor and on to
Arthur's Seat, marked with a simple cairn.
From here it is about 1km up to the top of
Hart Fell and, on the final approach, hop
over the fence and bear left to the trig
point marking the 808m summit of this
Corbett (a little short of a Munro). Time
for a pitstop, so pause and enjoy the fine
panorama across Moffat Water, Eskdale
and the Ettrick hills beyond.

Retrace the outbound route past
Arthur's Seat, over Billscleuch Moor and
again through the deer fence. Go
diagonally left, over the top of Newton
Fell, where the tussocky moorland, thick
with mosses and heather, makes for hard
walking. Start to drop down the hillside,
gradually curving right, picking up a kind
of gully-cum-track leading steeply down
off the hill. These lower slopes are now
planted with young tree saplings that will
perhaps one day recreate the thick forest
of Arthurian legend.

In the valley bottom, near Auchencat
Burn, turn right along the track, ford the
Spa Well Burn (the clue is in the name!)
and, after about 50m, turn right onto a
rough path leading up into the scree-lined
valley and Hartfell Spa. This chalybeate
spring, rich in iron and calcium, was
discovered in 1748 by John Williamson,
who was running a nearby mining
operation. The waters arguably healed
many ills, including 'debility and anaemia',
and were exported across the world.

Wander back to the main track, turn
right and follow this along the valley side
for about 3km to the start.

◀ Near the summit of Hart Fell

Moffat hills and spa heritage

Distance **8.5km** Time **2 hours 30**
Terrain **footpaths, open hills, grazing
fields** Map **OS Explorer 330** Access **parking
in Moffat centre (free); buses from
Dumfries, Glasgow and Lockerbie;
nearest train station at Lockerbie**

The spa town of Moffat was the place to
holiday in well-to-do Victorian Scotland.
Like the fashionable European *Kurorte*
(cure-towns) of Baden-Baden and
Carlsbad, the prosperous middle-classes
came to relax, soak in the Baths Hall
(now the Town Hall), play golf, tennis,
bowls and croquet, walk the hills,
socialise and drink the foul-smelling
sulphurous waters first discovered here in
1633. This route follows in their footsteps,
visiting the source of the town's healing
reputation on a tour of the local hills.

Start from the statue of a ram in the
High Street which celebrates the town's
wool trade history. Also known as the

Colvin Fountain it was designed by
William Brodie who was responsible for
the life-size bronze of Greyfriar's Bobby as
well as a number of other notable works
in Edinburgh.

Head north, passing the Stag pub and
pretty Eastgate before turning right just
after St Mary's church along Harthope
Place. Go left at the corner and slowly
wend your way uphill past the houses and
into the beechwood leading to Gallow Hill.
A magnificent 300-room Hydropathic
Hotel once stood below the track here but
closed as spa resorts fell out of fashion
and was destroyed by a fire in 1921.

Continue up the tree-lined track to
reach the handsome shingle-roofed
woodland shelter at the top, then go
through the two metal gates further on
and turn left. Now owned by the
community, Gallow Hill has been
replanted with native trees following
years of use as a sitka spruce plantation.

◀ The Moffat Ram

As the broad path rounds the corner look for a narrow path on the left. (If you get to a pair of round picnic benches you've gone too far.) Follow this to a gate and head diagonally right across the field to the next walkers' gate in the corner. Take a quick right and left onto a broad, firm track. Leave this just before Archbank plantation, climbing the sheep track off to the right and up over Hind Hill – waymarker posts lead the way to a fine view north to south from the Devil's Beeftub and on down Annandale.

Drop down off Hind Hill towards the cottage below, initially following a track, then the road downhill. Along the way nip off to the left at Well Cottage to visit Moffat Well. Today it is hard to picture this unprepossessing building, more akin to an eggy-smelling municipal bus shelter, being a hive of activity, but people once flocked here in their droves. The sulphurous water was usually 'taken' between 7 and 9am each day and offered 'cures' for all manner of ills. We don't recommend you try this today!

Further down the road, take the footpath left just before you reach the high bridge over Hind Gill, but not before peering over one of its ornate balconies into the deep gorge below. Follow the waymarker posts across the grazing fields and through a couple of gates before turning right at the track, then left at the sign labelled Rogermoor.

Carry on alongside the plantation and then take the path on the right across grazing fields and over burns, before joining a track which passes farmsheds and leads down to the Selkirk road. Off to the left on the way you'll see the enigmatic ruin of Frenchlands Tower, a reminder of the less genteel days of the Border Reivers when your home really had to be a castle. Turn right at the road to return to the High Street.

The Black Hope round

Distance 14km **Time** 5 hours 30
Terrain open hillside with bracken,
boggy sections and rough hill paths
Map OS Explorer 330 **Access** parking to
right of Blackshope cottages, taking care
not to block the gate/property; no public
transport to the start

Heart-pounding ascents, spectacular
scenery and precipitous ridges put this
horseshoe of hills up there with the best
in Southern Scotland. For hillbaggers,
a Corbett and three Donalds await:
Hart Fell, Swatte Fell, Hartfell Rig and
Under Saddle Yoke.

While the initial ascent can be a summer
battle with bracken, and a boggy section
two-thirds in tests the legs, the upper
levels are a joy, with firm grassy paths for
much of the length. Just a word on safety

– these paths can rapidly disappear in
poor visibility or snow, making map and
compass essential tools to avoid getting
too close to the numerous steep drops.

From Blackshope walk a short distance
back along the A708, crossing the
Blackhope Burn bridge and turning right
through a gate after the small building
and before the farmshed. Head towards
the ravine, through the gate and steeply
uphill following the course of the burn
and Hang Gill.

Continue between the waterfall and
cairn, through a gate, turning immediately
right and on through another gate. Bear
left and make the climb up over the top of
Black Craig, enjoying the sheer drop down
to the meandering Blackhope Burn far
below and views across the glen to Saddle
Yoke, reached later in the walk.

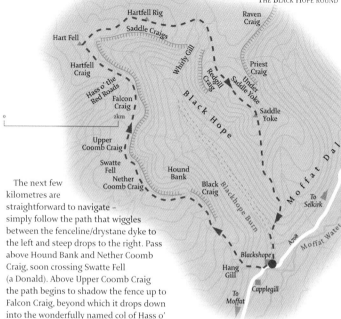

The next few kilometres are straightforward to navigate – simply follow the path that wiggles between the fenceline/drystane dyke to the left and steep drops to the right. Pass above Hound Bank and Nether Coomb Craig, soon crossing Swatte Fell (a Donald). Above Upper Coomb Craig the path begins to shadow the fence up to Falcon Craig, beyond which it drops down into the wonderfully named col of Hass o' the Red Roads. This marks the start of the push up to the walk's highest point, the trig point on Hart Fell (a Corbett).

Stay with the fence as it curves right across Hartfell Rig (a Donald) and down the other side. When the fence turns sharp left, leave it to go diagonally left on a faint path over the boggy hillside. Gradually arc right for the ascent of Under Saddle Yoke (another Donald). Be sure to keep above the headwater channels of Whirly Gill, but also be careful not to veer too far left. The route isn't always clear, which can make this section a slog through thick heather and bog.

At the top of Under Saddle Yoke (which is higher than Saddle Yoke) enjoy the fine vista all around. Cross the narrow, dramatic ridge to the next peak, Saddle Yoke, with Nether Torr Gill dropping steeply to the right and Carrifran to the left. At the cairn follow the clear path down across the spine of hills, nip over the fence-stile and continue upwards for the last climb of the day.

The path soon drops steeply to the right, eventually fading into the grassy slope. Continue down to meet the fence in the valley floor, go through the gate and back to the start.

◀ Blackhope Burn and surrounding hills

49

Carrifran Wildwood

Distance 4km **Time** 1 hour 30
Terrain rough footpaths, track and
boardwalk **Map** OS Explorer 330
Access small car park at Carrifran; no bus
service along Moffat Water

The ice-carved glen of Carrifran is the
site of a visionary Borders Forest Trust
project that has seen half a million trees
planted since 2000. Bears, wolves and lynx
once roamed here, picking off livestock
from the small nomadic groups that
moved through the hills and valleys with
the seasons. Today you won't find any
bears, but instead enjoy the wild drama
and isolation this spot offers – a true
taste of the Moffat Hills without too
much legwork.

From the small car park nip through the
kissing gate and head off to the right.

Follow this rough, sometimes muddy
path as it wends its way uphill to the
viewpoint in an old stone sheep fank.
Along the way a host of different tree
species, including aspen, rowan, juniper
and oak, are pointed out by information
markers – great in both winter and
summer for improving identification
skills – creating a beautiful and wildlife-
friendly mix of habitats.

Having soaked up the fine views all
around, drop down to the main track and
turn right to follow a linear 'in and out'
section along the course of the Carrifran
Burn. This simple and short amble packs
in plenty of big views, stunning scenery
and engaging history. Along the way keep
your eyes and ears open for a fulsome
range of wildlife: peregrine falcon and
raven swirl around the crags above, the

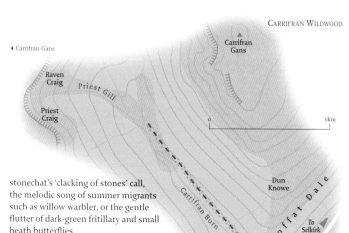

◀ Carrifran Gans

Carrifran Gans

Raven Craig

Priest Gill

Priest Craig

0   1km

Dun Knowe

Carrifran Burn

Moffat Dale

To Selkirk

footbridge

sheepfold

A708

Moffat Water

To Moffat

Carrifran

stonechat's 'clacking of stones' call, the melodic song of summer migrants such as willow warbler, or the gentle flutter of dark-green fritillary and small heath butterflies.

In winter and after rainy times this track can run like a burn in places, so be sure to wear sturdy, waterproof footwear. The roar of the Carrifran Burn accompanies you along this stretch and a very pleasant 30-minutes walking brings you to its gushing waters and stone cairn on the opposite bank. This is as far as this walk goes, so take a seat at the wooden bench and enjoy the seclusion the encircling hills provide. Up to the right is the craggy hillside of Raven Craig leading around to the evocatively named Rotten Bottom.

A broken hunting bow made of yew was found in the peat bog here in 1990. Dating back some 6000 years, it is the oldest surviving bow ever found in Britain but as yew did not grow so far north in those Neolithic times, the wood, or the bow itself, must have come from further south or Ireland. It now normally resides in the National Museum of Scotland but has been loaned to the local museum in Moffat just down the road.

Core samples taken from the bog uncovered preserved pollen charting the changes in vegetation since the last Ice Age and helped inform the present-day tree planting.

Retrace your steps back along the track and, when close to the viewpoint visited earlier, take the rough path downhill to the right. This eventually joins a boardwalk following the steep banks of the burn's ravine and provides fine views along Moffat Water. The path soon curves around to the left and returns to the start point.

Grey Mare's Tail and White Coomb

Distance 11.5km **Time** 5 hours
Terrain footpaths, boggy moorland and
steep hillside, also a tricky burn crossing
Map OS Explorer 330 **Access** parking at
NTS Grey Mare's Tail (charges for non-
members); no public transport to start

The Grey Mare's Tail Nature Reserve is
probably the nearest this region comes
to a tourist honeypot, but it's not hard to
escape the summer crowds. Most visitors
stop for a quick photo of one of the UK's
highest waterfalls; the bolder make the
one-hour climb up to beautiful Loch
Skeen; while the truly intrepid complete
the loch's backdrop of towering peaks,
which includes White Coomb, the
highest in Dumfriesshire.

This is a dramatic glacial landscape
forged from grinding ice, which today
hosts many natural rarities including
Britain's rarest fern, the oblong woodsia,
and rarest fish, the vendace. The crags

around the waterfall at the heart of this
National Trust for Scotland nature reserve
are home to the world's fastest animal,
the peregrine falcon and roaming wild
goats are the irresistible icing on this
outdoor cake.

From the car park cross the bridge and
immediately join the uphill pitched stone
footpath. Navigation is easy, simply stay
on this path up the side of the Grey
Mare's Tail, with its 60m drop, described
in Walter Scott's 1808 poem, *Marmion*, as
'White as the snowy charger's tail', and at
the top continue on through heather-
cloaked hills to Loch Skeen. Along the
way check the flow of the Tail Burn, the
crossing of which comes at the end of the
walk and can be particularly tricky after
rain or snowmelt.

Tranquil Loch Skeen is southern
Scotland's largest and highest natural
upland loch, sitting at some 500m above
sea level. The walking route around the

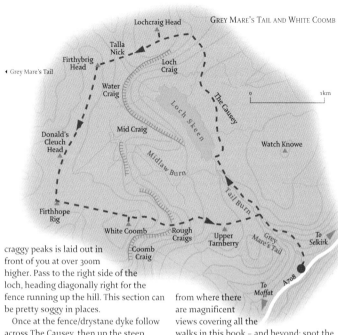

◀ Grey Mare's Tail

craggy peaks is laid out in front of you at over 300m higher. Pass to the right side of the loch, heading diagonally right for the fence running up the hill. This section can be pretty soggy in places.

Once at the fence/drystane dyke follow across The Causey, then up the steep climb of Lochcraig Head. To bag the summit proper nip over the stile for a 300m detour. Otherwise continue over the flat top, drop down to the col at Talla Nick and back up the other side to Firthybrig Head. Take a sharp left and stay with the dyke all the way to the wonderfully named Donald's Cleuch Head and then on up Firthhope Rig.

Take another sharp left and continue on for the final push up to the summit of White Coomb, but not before a testing drop of height over the intervening col. To reach the 821m summit veer right at the end of the fence up to the hilltop cairn

from where there are magnificent views covering all the walks in this book – and beyond: spot the distinctive hills of The Cheviot in Northumberland, Skiddaw in Cumbria, and the Eildon Hills near Melrose.

Retrace the route back to the dyke and follow to the right, dropping down off the hill. At the top of Rough Craigs leave the dyke for a short while to zigzag down the less steep section using the rough stone path. This soon re-joins the dyke for the onward section down to Tail Burn. Hop, jump or paddle across the burn, which might entail a bit of wandering upstream to find a suitable safe spot. Once back on the outbound path, turn right and follow downhill to reach the start.

The Bodesbeck ridge

Distance 12.5km **Time** 4 hours (one way)
Terrain rough tracks and open hillside
Map OS Explorer 330 **Access** leave one
vehicle parked carefully at Blackshope
and the second in a small pull-in near
Birkhill just over the county boundary;
no public transport to the start

**The peaks and cols between Trowgrain
Middle and Bodesbeck Law offer a
grandstand view across Moffat Dale to
Loch Skeen, White Coomb and Hart Fell.
This linear route travels from Birkhill to
Black Hope (which would require two
vehicles), but if you prefer to walk there
and back then simply turn around at
the top of Bodesbeck Law to retrace
your steps.**

From the roadside parking walk along
the A708 a short distance, stopping to

read the plaque on Birkhill Cottage
marking the pioneering graptolite fossil
studies by Victorian scientist Charles
Lapworth in nearby Dob's Linn. Just after
the cottage, turn left through the gate and
start the uphill climb on the distinct track
(there is a footpath sign before this taking
a higher route but at the cost of some of
the views).

Push on up the hillside, wending
around the top of Trowgrain Middle.
Across the glen Dob's Linn, complete with
waterfall, appears into view. At the top of
Raking Gill go through the wooden gate,
ford the burn and continue along the
uphill track. Along this stretch birdlife
abounds, from disgruntled black grouse
and melodic skylark to the summer treats
of wheatear (a more genteel name for the
16th-century 'white arse') and ring ouzel –
the mountain blackbird adorned with a

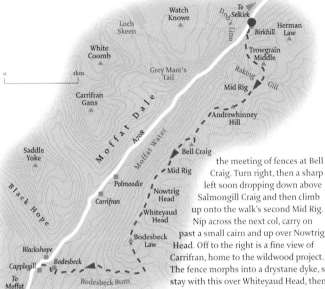

the meeting of fences at Bell Craig. Turn right, then a sharp left soon dropping down above Salmongill Craig and then climb up onto the walk's second Mid Rig. Nip across the next col, carry on past a small cairn and up over Nowtrig Head. Off to the right is a fine view of Carrifran, home to the wildwood project. The fence morphs into a drystane dyke, so stay with this over Whiteyaud Head, then go through the wooden gate and up to the cairn crowning the top of Bodesbeck Law.

If returning to the start on foot, simply turn around and retrace the outward route. For the linear walk follow the fence steeply down off Bodesbeck Law to the conifer wood and burn at the bottom of the col. Don't climb up the other side, instead turn right along the rough track wiggling down to Moffat Water along the burn. Continue on through a few gates, fording the burn a couple of times and finally going diagonally left through the valley bottom farmyard. At the track crossroads turn sharp right, go on up to the road and, with one last right turn, along to the finish at Blackshope.

fabulous white gorget (breast crescent).

Keep with the track up and over the first of the walk's Mid Rigs, through squelching mosses, and on up to the cairn on Andrewhinney Hill. Across to the right Loch Skeen and the famed Grey Mare's Tail Waterfall can now be seen, but for the best view drop slightly downhill. The large square-shaped hill is White Coomb, Dumfriesshire's highest.

Wander along the hillside eventually rejoining the fenceline, pass a low cairn and across the heather-cloaked col above Broken Cleuch. Head up the other side staying with the fence and continue up to

◀ Looking over Moffat Dale

Wamphray Glen

Distance 5km **Time** 2 hours
Terrain footpaths, farm fields and quiet
roads **Map** OS Explorer 322 **Access** parking
area by Wamphray Kirk; bus from Moffat
and Lockerbie, stopping at Newton
Wamphray (1.5km); nearest train station
is at Lockerbie

This circuit of idyllic Wamphray Glen
offers a fine taster of the Annandale
countryside, complete with lovely
views, gushing waterfalls, tempting wild
swimming spots and undulating paths
that twist and turn through ancient
woodland. Note that one section can
get very muddy in winter and after
heavy rain.

From the parking area head off past the
prettily situated Wamphray Kirk (visited
later in the route) and along the beech
hedge-lined lane, listening to the gushing
waters of Wamphray Water below. After
about 500m take the footpath on your
right climbing towards the woods and
crossing the ford over a small burn
flowing down Charter Cleuch.

A steady climb around woodland soon
opens up fine views of Queensberry Hill
with Harestanes windfarm in the
foreground. Follow the path around
Kirkhill farm, turning right at the hard
surface farm drive and then on down
to the road.

Take a quick left and right to reach a
pretty hedge-lined track that passes a
stand of mainly larch and offers views
across Annandale. Continue past the
farmhouse and at the road turn left,
taking the footpath on your right just
before the T-junction. This is the main
path into Wamphray Glen, a walking
route set up by the Crown Estate.
The glen is a tranquil spot, the sort of
place to sit and sketch or just while away
the stresses of everyday life.

The woodland here is technically

◄ Church sign in Wamphray Glen

described as ancient semi-natural, simply meaning it is old. The trees are locally native, occurring either through natural regeneration or coppicing and date back to map evidence of c1750. Simply follow the path for about 1.5km as it wends its way along the water, over bridges, up steps and around field edges. In a couple of places it is a bit storm damaged and hugs the hillside, but is still passable. Along the top, the route becomes a little less obvious but simply follow the fenceline along the field with a steep drop on your right. This leads past a fine waterfall, before crossing a wooden bridge where the Leithenhall Burn and Wamphray Water meet.

Turn right at the lane passing the old Mill and continue on through the contemporary kirkyard gate of brushed steel, the design of which invokes the wind, trees and water of the Glen.

The kirk was rebuilt on this site in 1834. Note the medieval carved foliate and monster on a stone lintel over the west door. Among the fine 19th-century funerary monuments is one to locally-born Dr John Rogerson, who became physician to the sexually voracious Catherine the Great – a role which included the dubious honour of checking her many lovers for venereal disease.

From here, leave the kirk and retrace a few steps back to the start.

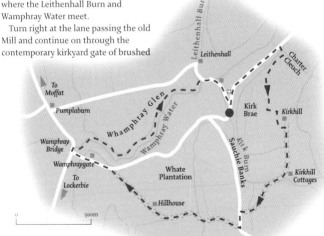

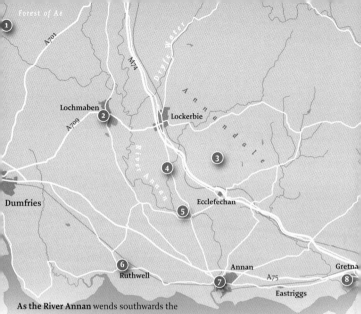

As the River Annan wends southwards the upland landscape gives way to the verdant rolling hills of Mid Annandale. Vast forests and glacial lochs pepper the undulations, hiding quirky secrets and fine views that many a traveller misses. Continue through Lower Annandale and these hills peter out as the land converges with the ever-shifting tides of the Solway Firth and the Scotland-England border.

The dale's north-south axis offered easy access for many invading forces across the centuries. The Romans, the English, squabbling clans and, more prosaically in recent times, even the scurry of non-native grey squirrels have all made this northwards incursion. On a more romantic note, this is also the land of eloping couples, who raced over the English border to Gretna Green to capitalise on Scotland's more relaxed marriage laws.

For some now, the rush north to the Scotland of a thousand postcards squeezes out all thought of this gentler landscape. But to miss this is to neglect not only the area's beauty and serenity, but also its dynamic place in history, for this land of once-mighty castles and border skirmishes has been instrumental in shaping the Scotland of today. Meanwhile, in the mix of lush fields, lochs, burns, forest and briny tides of the firth, wildlife abounds with playful otter, elusive willow tit, red squirrels and the swirling murmuration of starlings in their thousands.

Mid and Lower Annandale

Forest of Ae

Distance 9km **Time** 3 hour
Terrain forestry tracks and footpaths
Map OS Explorer 321 **Access** parking at
Forest of Ae car park (charges apply);
a few direct buses run from Dumfries,
more frequent services between
Moffat/Dumfries stop at Parkgate
(4km walk)

The village of Ae holds the honour of
having the shortest English place name
in the UK and also the only one without
any consonants. The Forest of Ae, and
the village with it, was born out of the
post-war drive to rebuild timber reserves,
but today is known for its world-class
7stanes mountain biking centre – not to
mention an enticing café.

A jaunt through Forestry Commission
Scotland's Forest of Ae encompasses
scenic pleasures, plenty of wildlife and
quirky oddities along the way. The

route is waymarked throughout with
brown markers on wooden posts, so
this is an easy walk to keep track of
(no pun intended).

Starting from the Forest Centre Café
and Bike Shop, step out on the path at the
back of the car park, turn right and then
left along the straight road with cattle
grids at either end. To the right is the
notorious field drop, the thrilling finalé of
the extreme-graded Ae downhill trail.
At the forest edge, the brown waymarkers
begin, so nip through the car park and
onto the footpath proper.

This first half of the walk meanders
along the babbling Water of Ae; a
tempting place to dip a toe and pause for
a while. The waterside path, at first shared
with mountain bikers, runs for about
2.5km, along the way crossing a bridge by
some lovely carved benches and then
turning immediately right to follow the

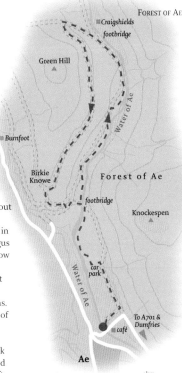

Craigshields
footbridge

Green Hill ▲

Water of Ae

◀ Squirrel sculpture in the Forest of Ae

Burnfoot ■

Birkie
Knowe

Forest of Ae

footbridge

Knockespen ▲

car
park

Water of Ae

To A701 &
Dumfries

● café ■

Ae

0   1km

other bank. After about 300m the path briefly wiggles away – just follow the markers and it soon rejoins the waterside.

The Water of Ae is a joy to wander alongside; pause and enjoy it as it flows downstream towards Kinnel Water and the River Annan beyond. Tree branches drip with mosses and in autumn a mass of red berries nourish hungry birds. If visiting in winter look out for the mysterious 'hair ice' – a candy-floss-like concoction which only grows in the presence of the *Exidiopsis effuse* fungus when the thermometer hovers just below zero and the air is humid.

Leaving the waterside path, turn right onto the main forestry track by an intriguing collection of forestry ploughs. The collection charts the development of tree planting technology and is not marked on any maps or leaflets.

Carry on along the main forestry track for about 1km, keeping your eyes peeled for the waymarker post guiding you left onto a narrow, rough uphill path. Follow the path as it bends sharp left towards the top and at another forestry track turn left to head around Green Hill. If you're ready for a break, there's a welcome bench here from which to enjoy the vista of Queensberry Hill from the Craigshields Viewpoint. From here you also get a real feel for the different forestry stages, from the newly planted whips (an unbranched sapling) through to maturing

trees and patches recently felled.

Continue on this main track for about 2km; towards the end it curves right and at a T-junction follow the track sharply down to the left. Continuing downhill, the brown markers guide you back to the Water of Ae bridge crossed earlier, from where retrace your steps back to the café – the perfect end to a lovely walk.

Lochmaben and Castle Loch

Distance 5km **Time** 1 hour 30
Terrain footpaths, pavement and quiet
roads **Map** OS Explorer 322 **Access** Loch
side car park behind the bowls club;
buses from Lockerbie and Dumfries;
nearest train station at Lockerbie

The Royal Burgh of Lochmaben is a
peaceful place, but scratch the surface
and you'll soon discover its pivotal role in
Scotland's often turbulent history. The
Romans, Iron Age settlers, King Edward I,
Robert the Bruce, King James V and Mary,
Queen of Scots have all played a part in
the town's story.

This easy walk centres on Castle Loch, is
fully waymarked with wooden fingerposts
and each footstep unlocks tales of those
stormier days. The loch is the largest of
the area's glacial kettle holes formed
some 15,000 years ago by blocks of ice
separating from the main glacier and
eventually melting to leave water-filled

depressions. The loch is surprisingly
shallow, only 5.5 metres at its deepest.

From the car park pass into Victory Park
and follow the first waymarker through
the sailing club, turning right at the road.
The route quickly enters the loch's
woodland fringe, crosses a car park and
continues on past Lochfield Cottage. The
cottage is the base for the community
trust which purchased the site in 2014 and
is the centre for their regular events and
volunteering activities.

Continue on into the woodland carr, an
increasingly rare wetland habitat, and
look out for the elusive willow tits that
frequent these parts. Cross over the burn,
keeping an eye open for a flash of blue
from a kingfisher, before following the
track and then footpath around the open
grassland to Valison Burn. On warm
summer days look out for azure and
variable damselflies buzzing over the
waters. They were previously believed not

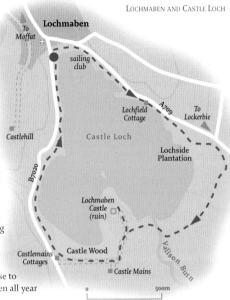

◀ Bruce carving by Castle Loch

to occur at the same location until this spot disproved the theory.

Cross the bridge and carry on along the boardwalk (sometimes flooded after prolonged heavy rains), nipping down to the bird hide on the right for fine views over the loch to Lochmaben and Queensberry Hill behind. In summer look out for visiting osprey and swirling sand martins, while in winter there are wildfowl such as pintail, tufted duck and geese to be spotted. Otters can be seen all year around – if you're lucky!

At the end of the boardwalk go up the short incline to the ruins of Lochmaben Castle. Today, this once mighty fortress built by King Edward I of England in 1298 is a far-from-impregnable pile of stones, but over 300 years the English and Scots fought many times to take control of it. In 1542 James V mustered his forces here before his English campaign, but with the Union of the Crowns between Scotland and England the need for such a defence disappeared and the castle was eventually abandoned in the 1700s. Local belief has it that much of the fascia stone which was carted away from the castle can now be seen in Lochmaben's houses!

Follow the track away from the castle (spot the carving of Robert the Bruce, the 7th Lord of Annandale as well as the King of Scots, among the trees) and on past the farm entrance, then take the right hand footpath into the woods, where local children regularly make use of the forest school areas. This woodland trail eventually leads back to the car park and is lined with a happy array of wooden carvings, including a woodpecker, otter and heron – take a peek behind each for more information.

Once back at the start, pop along to Lochmaben High Street with its fine buildings, cafés and pubs, and statues of the Burgh's great and good.

Burnswark Hill

Distance 6.5km **Time** 2 hours 30
Terrain farm tracks and hill paths (cattle
and livestock on lower slopes)
Map OS Explorer 322 **Access** parking at
Tundergarth Church; bus from Lockerbie
(request stop when boarding); nearest
train station is at Lockerbie

The brooding presence of Burnswark Hill
dominates the Solway plain in the mid-to-
lower reaches of Annandale. Visible from
all directions, it beckons not just walkers
but also archaeologists, for it was here on
this flat-topped hill around 140AD that the
Romans built a fort, having defeated the
Caledonian Selgovae tribe in what may
have been their first assault on Scotland.
This walk climbs gradually from the start
with just one steep section.

Start from Tundergarth Kirk, behind
which lies a small building that holds a
painfully moving book of remembrance

for those killed in the Lockerbie disaster
of 21 December 1988. Sitting here today in
this peaceful place it is hard to imagine
the horror of that night.

From the kirk parking area, walk down
the drive and continue ahead between the
house on the left and farm buildings on
the right. As the drive becomes a track,
follow it uphill to the left behind the
house and then keep ahead for around
1km with views of Burnswark to the right.
On reaching a gate and drystane dyke,
head right across the field (before passing
through the gate), signed Burnswark,
following the line of the wall on your left.
Livestock may be present here, so keep
dogs on a lead and give cows with calves a
wide berth.

At the end of the first field, go left
through the gate and then right, still
following the line of the dyke, now on
your right, passing into the next field and

then along the edge of woodland, to reach a couple of farm byres. Immediately past the byres, bear left on the track and, before reaching the stand of trees on the left, go right uphill between a dyke and a fence.

Where the dyke turns left, strike out up the hill, directly south, aiming for the cleft in the middle of the hill, with ever-expansive views opening up behind. At the top of the cleft, go left to reach the cairn and to take in the glorious panorama of Annandale to the north, the Langholm hills to the east, the Solway to the south and Criffel to the west.

Return to the top of the cleft and turn left, picking up the path which heads over to the gates diagonally on the right. Go through the right hand gate and then turn immediately left to follow the track as it contours the hill down to the right. As the path comes round the base of the hill, head west, aiming for an avenue of trees around 350m away at the edge

of the field. (If in doubt, follow the line of the drystane wall over to the left down to the bottom of the field and then turn right along the line of the wall.)

On reaching the trees, turn right and keep ahead to go through a gate. Continue forward for just under 1km on a track which runs alongside woodland on the right to return to the farm byres passed earlier, from where the outward route can be retraced back to the start.

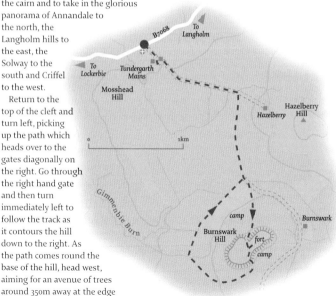

Old St Mungo's and the Water of Milk

Distance 8km **Time** 2 hours 30
Terrain tracks and quiet country roads
Map OS Explorer 322 **Access** parking by
kirkyard gates (please don't obstruct the
gates); no public transport to the start

**This walk linking two atmospheric ruins
wanders along quiet roads and woodland
tracks between the parallel waters of the
River Annan and delightfully named
Water of Milk. All around is rolling
countryside, surprisingly hilly at times,
with fine views up and down Annandale.**

The start point is the small ruin of the
12th-century St Mungo's kirk, sitting
alone on a knoll on the north bank of the
river. The kirk was donated by the Bruce
family to the bishops of Glasgow, hence
its dedication: St Mungo is the patron
saint and founder of the City of Glasgow.
Today the only remnant of any substance
is the east gable wall, housing numerous
dedications to the Jardine family who hail

from these parts; the best known
being Lochmaben-born William Jardine,
opium trader and co-founder of Jardine
Matheson, the successful Hong Kong-
based trading dynasty.

Firstly, pop into the old kirkyard to
explore the ruins and fine stone
monuments to former residents of the
area. When leaving the old kirkyard turn
right along the lane, passing the parking
area, and take the next lane right uphill
passing Kirkbank Farm and around the
sharp S-bends, with views to the right
down to the River Annan.

Continue down the long straight
lane edged with an old gorse hedge,
turning right by the woodland strip,
signed Annandale Way. This lovely lane is
lined with a fine beech hedge and a
babbling burn lush with overhanging
verdant mosses and offers views to
Repentance Tower on a distant hilltop.

Continue ahead as the lane becomes a

◀ Ruins of Milkbank House

track (muddy after wet weather) by a young willow woodland, then following it around to the left at the far end of the wood (signed Annandale Way – via Lockerbie). Reaching the lane, the rushing Water of Milk can be heard ahead; turn left here and continue up to the road. Cross straight over onto the estate track by the lodge, but not before looking for dipper, doing exactly as its name suggests, from the river bridge to your right. The estate entrance still has signs of its former grandeur; look for a once-fine wall now tumbled and the ornate wrought iron gates clad in a jacket of thick ivy.

Follow the track, abuzz with butterflies on warm sunny days, to the romantic ruins of Milkbank House nestling in the woods in a commanding position overlooking a sweeping bend of the Water of Milk. Built in the Scottish Baronial style, what remains is a heady mix of crow-stepped gables, turrets, hanging fireplaces and porte cochère (carriage porch), and today it makes for a magical if unexpected find.

Carry on past the ruins and turn left at the T-junction with the lane, continuing on up the hill. Off to the right the views soon open up. Look out for glimpses of the newer St Mungo's kirk of 1877 in

Kettleholm and bare, flat-topped Burnswark Hill on the skyline.

Pass the cottages, painted in the distinctive white and dark green of the Castlemilk Estate, and at the crossroads leave the Annandale Way to turn left, passing around 300m further on Hilltop House and skirting Nutholm Hill. From here enjoy the far-reaching views along the River Annan valley before dropping back down to the start point.

Hoddom Castle and Repentance Tower

Distance 7km **Time** 2 hours
Terrain footpaths, fields and quiet
roads **Map** OS Explorer 322 **Access** car park
close to Hoddom bridge; bus from
Gretna, Lockerbie and Annan to
Hoddom Cross (1.5km)

History, wildlife, far-reaching views and a
grizzly tale or two await on this pleasant
stroll on the Hoddom and Kinmount
estate. There's one optional steep section
– but it's worth the huff and puff to reach
the Repentance Tower. At the top rest a
moment on a tomb (the occupants don't
seem to mind) and take in views
stretching over the Solway Firth to the
Cumbrian mountains.

Turn right out of the car park following
the road fringed with woodland and
carpeted in ransoms (wild garlic) and
bluebells during the spring, and foxgloves
and campion in summer. After about 1km
take the uphill path on the left leading to

Repentance Tower, built by Sir John
Maxwell, 4th Lord Herries, during the
1560s as a watchtower for his nearby
Hoddom Castle. Encircled by a large
drystane dyke, the tower is surrounded
by many impressive 17th-century
gravestones. Quite why 'Repentance' is
carved over the tower's entrance is lost to
history; many a tall story rumbles around
this ancient beacon hill and the most
popular are outlined on the information
board at the foot of the tower.

Retrace your steps to the road, turn left
and after about 100m take the unmarked
track on the right down through the
woods and heading diagonally right
across the caravan park towards the ruins
of Hoddom Castle. Sir John was Warden of
the Scottish West March and this was his
central stronghold. However, the 1603
Union of the Crowns brought a
quietening of border hostilities and less
need for a defensive fortress. With World

◀ Repentance Tower

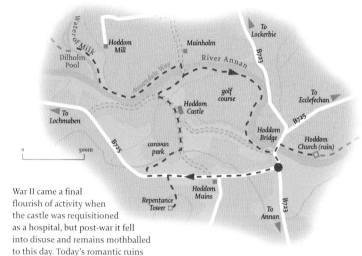

War II came a final
flourish of activity when
the castle was requisitioned
as a hospital, but post-war it fell
into disuse and remains mothballed
to this day. Today's romantic ruins
provide a great backdrop for family
holidays and just past the castle the
Victorian stableyard is now home to the
dog-friendly Coach House Bar, complete
with vaulted ceiling and resident horse
(plastic) and carriage.

Continue on for about 100m and then
turn right following the track down
through the woods, over the wooden
steps and down to the River Annan. For
an interesting detour cross the river
bridge and turn left to follow the riverside
salmon trail, telling a fishy tale from egg
to adult. At the 'eggs in gravel wall' turn
around and wander back, looking out for
goosander and otter along the way. Cross
back over the bridge and turn left to

follow the meandering river around
the golf course and into the woods. When
the path splits keep ahead along the river
to the gatehouse.

Crossing the fine stone bridge, built in
the 1760s to replace the boat ferry, take
the footpath immediately on the right
leading to a riverside kirkyard dedicated to
St Kentigern or Mungo, patron saint and
founder of the City of Glasgow, who is
said to have lived as Bishop here in the
7th century. All that remains of this once
monastic site is a higgledy-piggledy mix
of fascinating carved gravestones.

Retrace your steps back over the bridge
and through the castle drive gates to take
the footpath on the left to the car park.

Ruthwell and the Cross

**Distance 7km Time 2 hours
Terrain footpaths, merse (saltmarsh)
and quiet roads (cattle graze the merse)
Map OS Explorer 322 Access parking on
the rough track to the side of Brow Well;
buses from Dumfries and Carlisle;
nearest train stations are at Annan
and Dumfries**

**From immense skies, framed with
sweeping Solway merse and distant
Cumbrian mountains, to the home of
the world's first savings bank and a
gigantic stone cross from the Dark Ages,
the unassuming parish of Ruthwell
rewards those who take time to explore
this flatter corner of Dumfriesshire.**

Today the seeping chalybeate spring of
Brow Well tempts few visitors to try a cure
for their ills, but throughout the 1700s the
waters were a busy stop off for those who
believed in its 'healing qualities'. Robert
Burns visited in 1796 to ease his 'flying
gout' by drinking the iron-salt water and
bathing in the Solway, but to no avail as
he died shortly afterwards.

Take the track alongside the well and
out on to the merse, part of the
Caerlaverock National Nature Reserve.
This mass of watery channels is a sea of
flowers throughout spring and summer
and offers fine views south to Cumbria
and west to Criffel, the area's largest hill.
The reserve is home to many birds and
animals, some of which, like the
natterjack toad, are very rare. Others, such
as barnacle geese and whooper swans, can
be seen here in their thousands when
they arrive for the winter, making this a
walk for all seasons.

Wend your way across wooden bridges,
hopping watery channels as you go. In
summer cattle graze, so be aware of the
electric fence, cross using the stile and
give them a wide berth, particularly if
walking with a dog. The path curves left
and becomes increasingly indistinct, with

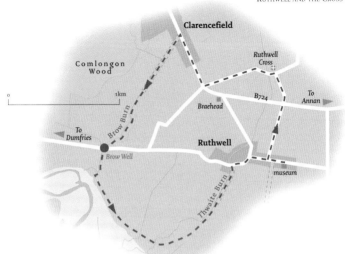

ever fewer waymarkers for guidance, but keep heading diagonally left for the metal gates and the hedgeline of weather-beaten hawthorn. This section can be a bit muddy at times, particularly after inclement weather.

Follow the grassy track away from the coast and at the road turn right into Ruthwell, a small village of single-storey white-painted stone cottages. About 500m along the main street lies a quirky and memorable treat – a 200-year-old cottage and site of the world's first savings bank opened in 1810. Today it is home to the Savings Banks Museum (free), run by friendly staff who bring to life the story of the altruistic Dr Henry Duncan, minister, author, antiquarian, geologist, publisher, artist and philanthropist. One highlight is a wonderful collection of moneyboxes.

Retrace your steps back along the main street, turning right at the first turn and, after a few minutes, go straight over the crossroads and down to Ruthwell Kirk. If the doors are locked the key can be collected from the neighbours. Inside stands the Ruthwell Cross, a 7th-century Anglo Saxon preaching cross, unusually carved with both Latin and runic inscriptions, which is the oldest of its kind on mainland UK.

Turn right on leaving the kirk to follow the lane uphill and at the next road turn right up in to Clarencefield village, popping into the Farmers Inn for refreshments. Take the footpath opposite the Old Police Station, passing the playing fields and continuing into the woods to follow the babbling Brow Burn back to the start.

◀ On the merse of the Solway

Annan and the Solway

Distance 8km **Time** 2 hours 30
Terrain pavement, footpaths and merse
(saltmarsh) **Map** OS Explorer 322
Access parking in Annan town centre;
buses from Dumfries, Carlisle and
Lockerbie; train station at Annan

Unlock Annan's colourful past on a
walk that sets out from the town's
handsome sandstone civic buildings.
The town's proximity to England led to
many a skirmish in the area during the
Wars of Independence and among reiving
families on either side of the border, but
in times of peace Annan prospered
through agriculture, fishing, shipping
and engineering. This walk also visits
the site of a lost railway viaduct, with a
hop, skip and a few jumps over the
watery channels of the Solway Firth
merse to finish.

Starting from the Scottish baronial
Town Hall, close to the river bridge,
wander eastwards along the broad
curving High Street lined with shops. Pass
the Old Parish Church and turn right
down Solway Street, then go on through
Hecklegirth with its fine sandstone villas
and over the railway bridge. Just after the
timber plant take the steps up on to the
old railway embankment, now a footpath
lined with hawthorn and elder, and,
turning right, follow it to its abrupt end
jutting out into the Solway Firth. Between
1869 and 1934, the Solway Viaduct crossed
these treacherous waters from Bowness
on the English side and was mainly used
to transport iron ore to the steelworks
in Lanarkshire.

Retrace your steps about 500m then
turn left to follow the waymarker arrows
off the old railway bed and along the

◀ Looking over the Solway

raised dyke. Look out for flocks of lapwing swirling overhead, geese grazing alongside the resident sheep and steres of driftwood washed in on many a stormy tide.

At Summergate Lane (signed Annan) keep straight ahead and drop down on to the merse for a kilometre of 'dub' jumping, dub being the Scottish word for pool, especially if it's muddy and full of stagnant or sea water. Head for the line of benches along the merse edge and then follow your nose to Waterfoot. Most of the dubs are easy to step over but at the four larger watery channels head back inland to find a point narrow enough to leap across with care. On a clear day enjoy the fine views of the Cumbrian mountains, while literally right in front of you can be hundreds, if not thousands, of wading birds calling, arguing and probing the Solway mud for a tasty morsel.

The channels peter out at the mouth of the River Annan, at an area called Waterfoot, a once prosperous port from where schooners set sail for North America. Robert Burns knew this area well as he spent the last years of his short life here in his less poetic role as a 'gauger' or exciseman checking arriving cargo.

Follow the tarmac lane away from Waterfoot, over the cattle grid and at the cottages at Waterfoot Road turn left down to Annan Harbour. Today the quay is a far cry from the bustle of its Georgian and Victorian heyday, although traces of shipping and fishing do remain and the Annan Harbour Action Group is working hard to rejuvenate the surrounding area as a community asset.

Turn right to walk up Port Street and back to the town centre. While here it's worth popping into the interesting Annan Museum on Bank Street (free entry).

Gretna and the border

Distance 12.5km **Time** 4 hours
Terrain footpaths, fields and quiet
roads **Map** OS Explorer 323
Access car park on Central Avenue;
buses from Dumfries and Carlisle;
train station at Gretna Green

**Even if you know little of Dumfriesshire,
Gretna Green is sure to conjure romantic
images of young love and frantic carriage
dashes. Yet the area has a much more
complicated story to tell, which is
revealed in this walk of love, tragedy
and bloody border warfare.**

Gretna and Gretna Green are two
distinct villages, so starting from the
centre of the former turn right out of the
car park up Central Avenue. Gretna was
built during World War I to house some
30,000 munitions workers and was
designed using the then in-vogue
principles of Garden Cities.

Go straight across at the traffic lights
and at the top join Mackies Drive then the
footpath heading through a tunnel and

up to Gretna Green. Cross the road, go
under the A74(M) and up to the Famous
Blacksmiths Shop where the tradition of
mixing business and weddings continues
unabated. The museum, with its famous
anvil, is worth a visit – and there's a fair
chance of seeing a wedding too.

Take the quiet lane to the left of the
Blacksmiths and wander along for about
1.5km. Pause at Blacksike Bridge and take
a look along the railway line towards
Quintinshill, where on 22 May 1915,
215 soldiers, 9 passengers and 3 railway
employees were killed in Britain's worst
rail disaster, a tragedy little reported due
to wartime restrictions. The soldiers were
mainly volunteers from the 7th Royal
Scots from Leith bound for Gallipoli.

Continue for a further 400m, then turn
right along the 'Public Path' (signed
Springfield). Go past the farm and right at
the next 'Public Path' sign down a lovely
track lined with hawthorn and towering
beech. Head up the slight incline to
Quintinshill Bridge, pass the bench and at

◀ The Old Blacksmith's Shop in Gretna Green

the lane turn left. Cross over the railway once more and at the left bend turn right through a gate and along the field edge (sometimes muddy and sometimes with livestock). Go under the railway and up the track to the Queen's Head pub in Springfield. Many of the area's inns benefited from the 'runaway wedding' trade, triggered by changes in English marriage laws during the 18th century, which decreed that couples had to be 21 to wed without parental consent. Scotland's more relaxed approach led to local inns paying couriers to bring couples across the border.

Cross the road and follow the track. Go through the gate and left around the field edge, through a kissing-gate, left again and through another gate above Hustle Bank. Drop down to the River Sark and, staying with the river bank, go under the M74(M) and around to the Old Toll Bar, 'the first (and last) house in Scotland'.

Cross the busy road and meander along the riverside path, through the gap in the dismantled railway and down to meet the Solway. Continue along the merse (saltmarsh), jumping the channels, for about 1km to the cottage at Stormont. (If the going is too tough, head towards the

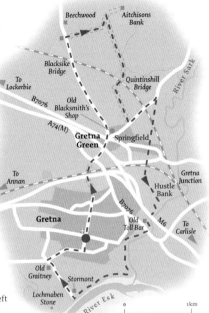

top of the merse just after the large house and follow the fenceline.)

Turn right up the lane at Stormont, crossing the site of the 1448 Battle of Sark, where a 6000-strong English army was routed and pushed back into the rising Solway tide by a much smaller muster of Annandale and Nithsdale men. After Auld Graitney turn right and head back into Gretna on Empire Way, turning left opposite the small park and walking back up Central Avenue to the start.

Eskdalemuir

From the isolation of Eskdalemuir's rolling hills in the north to the flatter lands of Canonbie's historic 'Debatable Lands' in the south, Eskdale is a land of contrasts. Like so much of the Scotland-England borderland, this region was historically much disputed. For over three hundred years up until the Union of the Crowns in 1603, Eskdale's southern reaches were a no-man's land, where the only loyalty was to your clan, with the Armstrongs, on the Scottish side of the Border, being the most prominent.

Today the seasons pass and little seems to change. Spring flowers give way to harsher winter landscapes via summer's haze of heather-cloaked hills and autumn's golden umbers. Topography influences the dale's outlook, where access points and historic ties engender greater affinity with the Scottish Borders to the east and Carlisle to the south rather than with the official administrative home of Dumfries and Galloway.

This is a watery landscape of rivers, burns, bogs and rain, lots of rain – some 60cm more each year than in neighbouring Annandale and up to 22 wet days per month in the summer. Indeed, it was partly thanks to such intemperate consistency that Langholm's many

Langholm

Eskdale River Esk

Canonbie

historic cloth and woollen mills sprang up, capitalising on the town's rivers and its proximity to the cotton mills of Carlisle and earning the town the nickname of the 'Muckle Toon' ('Big Town').

Alas the mills are now gone, but in their place have come artisans creating works inspired by the hills, and community-based initiatives eager to welcome visitors. At Eskdalemuir there is also the unexpected sight of the first Tibetan Buddhist centre established in the west.

These quiet hills and glens are characterised by ancient hillforts, stone circles, lonely steadings and, more recently, commercial forestry. Sure, it can be damp, but with the right gear this is a land to savour.

Eskdale

Eskdalemuir hills and temple

Distance 14km **Time** 4 hours 30
Terrain quiet roads, tracks and open
hillside (cattle and livestock in lower
fields) **Map** OS Explorer 323
Access parking at the Eskdalemuir
Community Hub; buses from
Langholm and Lockerbie

The quiet village of Eskdalemuir was
once the preserve of sheep farmers
and meteorologists, but today is an
unexpected fusion of eastern and
western culture. A kirk and stone bridge
stand proud at its heart, but all around
colourful prayer flags hint at the more
recent addition of eastern spirituality.

Start from the rejuvenated Old School,
now a thriving community hub with shop
and café. Turn left out of the car park and
follow the road past the church and over
the river. As the main road curves right
continue straight ahead down the lane –
becoming a track – to Clerkhill Farm, then
follow the footpath signs left and right
around the farm.

Cross the field, go through a kissing
gate and along the fence, soon to join the
track up into the quiet glen. After about
1km take the lower, right hand track by
the stock fencing and sheep fank. Ford the
burn and continue around Windshiel Rig,
taking the right hand path uphill at the
fork. Don't go through the gate in front of
the conifer plantation, instead turn left
and follow the fence to the summit of
Grey Hill. From here it's 1.5km of rough
hillside, all squelching mosses and
ankle-turning tussocks, so tread carefully,
but also enjoy the cracking views over to
the Ettrick Hills.

Once at the top of Grey Hill strike off down the open hillside in a rough northwesterly (diagonally left) direction, eventually to pick up the track down to the dwellings at Rae Burn. By the red-roofed barn go diagonally right over the field, on through the gate with the fingerpost, following the burn to cross a bridge and continue down the track.

At the T-junction turn right and walk over the hill to Moodlaw. Just before the house turn left at the track crossroads, go down between the woods and past an intriguing caravan. Stay on the track, keeping to the left side of the fence at the old Bedford van, and carry on through a wooden gate by the river. The Samye Ling Tibetan monastery sits serenely on the opposite bank, offering a most unexpected vista of colourful buildings, robed monks and mighty yaks. Established in 1967, the monastery was the first of its kind in the west and has attracted some famous visitors over the years; Leonard Cohen and David Bowie were both students here for a time and John Lennon and Yoko Ono were also frequent visitors in the early days.

Continue left along the rough river

bank and through another wooden gate, then turn right to stay briefly with the fence before curving left along the bottom of the hill. Scramble in front of the small stand of conifers, over the burn and up the other side. Continuing across the fields, go through a couple of gates and join the track to Raeburnfoot Farm, passing the site of two Roman Forts (one inside the other) as you go.

After the farm cross the burn and follow the access track all the way back to Clerkhill Farm, then retrace the outbound route back to the start to enjoy a refreshing pitstop in the Old School, followed by some quiet contemplation at Samye Ling.

◀ Above the White Esk

Bessie's Hill and Castle O'er

Distance 9km **Time** 3 hours
Terrain forestry tracks and rough
footpaths **Map** OS Explorer 323
Access parking at Bessie's Hill; buses
from Langholm and Lockerbie stop in
Eskdalemuir village (3km walk)

The rolling hills of the upper reaches of
Eskdale, just a stone's throw from
Eskdalemuir, are swathed in forestry
plantation which conceals a history
spanning millennia. Once these lands
were populated by the Selgovae tribe,
rulers of much of southwest Scotland
– today the mighty hilltop grass banks
and deep ditches of Bessie's Hill and
Castle O'er are all that remain.

Impressive in location, there is still
enough here to make for a good clamber

and to give some inkling of what a huge
effort it must have taken to create these
Iron Age settlements and forts in such an
isolated spot. This is an undemanding
route, both underfoot and to navigate,
mostly on hard surface tracks provided by
Forestry Commission Scotland, with only
a couple of rougher path sections.

From Bessie's Hill car park head back
towards the road and take the footpath
off left, marked with a blue waymarker
post, up through woods lush with mosses
to the main track. For the best views walk
up to the settlement site on the crown of
the hill, then retrace your steps and head
along to explore the mounds of the
hillfort. Once finished continue on the
forestry track, with its fine views down
over Eskdale or, depending on conditions,

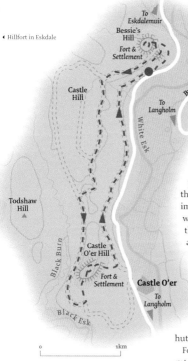

◀ Hillfort in Eskdale

of this section the blanket of dark conifer trees begins to thin, revealing glimpses of Black Burn babbling down to the right, while to the left is the peak topped by Castle O'er. The forestry track curves left around the heathery hillside and where it bends sharp right head off to the left indicated with the yellow waymarker post. At this point then take the rough footpath immediately on the left, again indicated with the yellow marker, and continue through the heather. Go over the stile and up to the top of the hill, where the mighty grassy banks and ditches of Castle O'er are clear to see – and from where the huge size of the modern-day forestry operation becomes clear. Sit a while, enjoy the 360 degree views, and try to visualise the 30 round, wooden, thatched huts once protected by these defences.

Follow the rough path down and, if the gate is closed, go over a large wooden stile crossing the same fence climbed over on the way up. At the forestry track go left and stay with it as it curves left (don't follow the yellow waymarker right as this just leads to a car park).

Stay with this lower track, which is more open than the outbound route and offers numerous views along Eskdale, for about 2km. At the track T-junction turn right and head downhill back to the start.

looking down on an atmospheric shroud of mist coating the valley below.

The track re-enters the forest and at the T-junction go left, shortly arriving at another track junction, at which veer to the right. After about 1.5km the track bends around to the right heading gently downhill. At the next track junction turn left and continue straight through the forest for just over 1km. Towards the end

Arkleton Hill and Ewes Valley

Distance 11km Time 4 hours
Terrain track and open hillside
Map OS Explorer 323 Access parking at
Ewes Hall; buses from Langholm and
Hawick/Galashiels

The vista from the top of Arkleton Hill
out over Ewesdale, down Eskdale and to
the Solway Firth beyond is one of
Dumfriesshire's best-kept secrets.
There's no denying that this is a
strenuous route once off the main
tracks – peatbogs with perilous gullies,
tussocky grasses and a lack of any
obvious paths – but don't be deterred,
peace, isolation, majesty and plenty of
wildlife reward the intrepid walker.

From Ewes Hall cross the main road and
head down the track, passing Sandyhaugh
Cottages and crossing the bridge
spanning Ewes Water. Follow the long
straight track on past a huge walled

garden, then a left, right and left chicane
through Arkleton farmyard. Look out to
the left for glimpses of Arkleton House.
This was once the home of MP Walter
Scott-Elliot and his wife, Dorothy, who
in 1977 were murdered by their servant,
Archibald Hall in a convoluted tale of
skulduggery too complex to explain here.
However, the tabloids soon nicknamed
him 'the Monster Butler'.

Initially the route climbs gently out into
open countryside, soon reaching a fork.
Keep right here, passing a small waterfall
and wending uphill for a couple of
kilometres. At the gate by the newly
planted wood, all a mass of protective
tubes, don't go through but instead cross
the stile to the left.

This is the start of the ankle-testing,
heart-pumping, heavy-breathing section.
As a bonus, it's also choc-a-bloc with
mewing buzzard, frolicking wild goats,

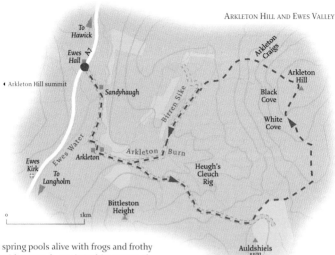

◄ Arkleton Hill summit

spring pools alive with frogs and frothy with spawn, bouncing white rumps of roe deer, darting stoat, summer's purple heather and, even in late winter, the song of skylarks.

Follow the fenceline around the new wood and, after about 500m, when the fence takes a sharp right turn, keep straight ahead, climbing and squelching up the hillside. There are some old waymarker posts, but to the left of these is a faint path which makes for easier going.

With head down and concentrating on each footstep, you might miss the views, so take a well-earned breather and have a look around, enjoying distant views down Ewesdale and over the Newcastleton Hills. Turn left to follow the fenceline uphill for a further 1km or so, above the craggy White Cove and Black Cove outcrops. When the cairn is in sight leave the fence and strike off over heather and deep

boggy gullies to reach the walk's highest spot.

Pause to soak up the panorama and recharge the batteries with a pitstop. When ready, continue ahead in the same direction, turning left at the fence and carefully descending the steep slope. At the bottom cross the stile and head diagonally left passing the sheep fank and joining the prominent track beyond.

Go left along the track which follows the course of the Birren Sike and Arkleton Burn and continue on up a final steep section. The track eventually rejoins the earlier outbound route; simply turn right and follow it back through Arkleton farmyard and down to Ewes Hall.

While exploring Ewesdale, stop off at Ewes Kirk, just a short drive south, with its intriguing bell hanging in the cleft of a tree.

Whita Hill

Distance 8km **Time** 2 hours 30
Terrain tracks, rough moorland and quiet
roads (unsuitable for dogs March–May
when calving cattle are on the hills)
Map OS Explorer 323 **Access** parking at
Kilngreen car park (free); buses from
Galashiels, Selkirk, Carlisle and Lockerbie

**Stunning scenery and a steep climb
or two make the heart race on this
riverside and moorland wander.
Heading out of town along the pretty
Ewes Water, the route then climbs to the
top of Whita Hill above Langholm,
crowned with the prominent Malcolm
Monument obelisk.**

Looking down over Langholm from the
higher reaches it's obvious how the town
got its name – lang meaning 'long' and
holm, in Scots, denoting 'level land for
pasture, often by water'. It was here in the
late 19th and early 20th centuries that one
Christopher Murray Grieve was born and
educated – better known today as Hugh
Macdiarmid, poet, essayist, political figure
and one of the founding members of the
National Party of Scotland (today's SNP).

From the car park head away from town
and turn immediately left over the small
stone bridge. Bearing right at the
Buccleuch Estate office, follow the lane
uphill (signed Pathhead) and then, after

passing the bungalow, along the hedge-
lined track. The fine views up Ewes Water
make up for the mud underfoot.

After the metal gate turn right at the
end of the drystane dyke and go through
the kissing gate and along the field edge.
At the woods drop down left to the road,
turn right to carefully cross Highmill
Bridge and then go left onto the track
along Ewes Water. After about 500m the
track banks sharply right and as it peters
out nip down to the left crossing the Far
Whitshiels Cleuch, locally known as

To Hawick
A7
Ewes Water
Castle Hill
Whitshiels Bog
Far Whitshiels Cleuch
Highmill Bridge
Whitshiels Knowe
memorial
Charlie's Moss
Wattie's Bank
Pathhead
mill
Ewes Bridge
Langholm
B709
Whita Road
golf course
Whita Well
Whita Hill
monument
Whita Hill
0   1km
River Esk
A7
To Longtown

Target Burn after an old army firing range.

At the top of the steep climb go right and wiggle through the scrubby trees, cross the stile and turn right to follow the drystane dyke. At the waymarker post veer diagonally left between the remains of two low dykes, towards the distant pylons. This is rough walking, often boggy and overgrown, with no obvious path, but persevere and, just before the pylons, join a more distinct track heading to the right over hill and burns.

Don't go through the wooden gate, but instead follow the drystane dyke left under the pylons and up the rough hillside. At the road hop over the fence (no stile provided) and go left along the road to sculptor Jake Harvey's wonderful open book installation depicting imagery from Hugh MacDiarmid's works. Continue onwards up the broad track to the top of Whita Hill and a mighty monument to Sir John 'Boy' Malcolm, the son of a Langholm farmer who at the tender age of 12 joined the East India Company and rose through its ranks to become the Governor of Bombay.

From here take the waymarked path directly downhill towards Langholm and just before the pylon veer left to Whita Well with its chained metal drinking cup beckoning for a little sip. Carry on down the path, through a gate and along the Whita Road track. At Arkinholm Terrace, the place of MacDiarmid's birth, cross the road and go steeply downhill to the High Street, at which turn right and wander back, via the shops and cafés, to the start.

◀ The Malcolm Monument

Jenny Noble's Gill

Distance 8km **Time** 2 hours 30
Terrain pavement, footpaths, and quiet
lanes **Map** OS Explorer 323 **Access** parking
at Kilngreen car park (free); buses from
Galashiels, Selkirk, Carlisle and Lockerbie

With just a couple of short uphill
sections, this easy figure-of-eight route
has a watery feel, with a bit of town and
hillside thrown in for good measure.
Following the same outward route as the
Warb Law walk, it meanders along the
River Esk before nipping off over
Skipper's Bridge and onto an old railway
embankment. A brief flit across open
hills follows before doubling back to
climb the woodland path above Jenny
Noble's Gill and return to Langholm.

Leaving the car park turn right and then
first right over the River Esk. Take the first
left along Elizabeth Street, following the
road as it bears right to pass the parish
church on the left, and then turning left
over the footbridge into Buccleuch Park.
Head straight across the park onto the
Easton's Walk woodland footpath, go left
at the path junction to stay with the river
and follow the broad track until it
eventually meets the main A7 road.

Carefully cross Skipper's Bridge,
designed in 1807 by the 'Colossus of
Roads' Thomas Telford, the prodigiously
hardworking son of an Eskdale shepherd
who built dozens of roads, canals,
harbours and bridges all around Scotland,
England, Wales and Sweden. Turn
immediately right and climb the steep
steps to join the dismantled Border Union
Railway Branch Line, today a fabulous arch
of beech trees. Go through a kissing gate
and continue uphill wiggling through a
woodland of old oaks and silver birch.

Ahead is the Round House, visited later;
for now follow the path as it curves right

To Hawick

Langholm woodland

Langholm

Whita Hill

Charteris Craigs

River Esk

Easton's Walk

Carlin Gill

Murtholm

Skipper's Bridge

Round House

Long Wood

B6318

Jenny Noble's Gill

Longwood

Red Gill

Broomholmshiels

To Longtown

and right again onto a broader track. After about 500m continue ahead on the track, ignoring the wooden sign for Jenny Noble's Gill. The route eventually leaves the woodland for a stretch over open hillside of gorse and bracken, through a couple of gates and past Broomholmshiels Farm. Turn right at the small lane and right again along the quiet road, continuing for about 1km. This section is mainly a canopy of fine trees in summer or more open views of hills and river in winter, lined with a drystane dyke dripping in mosses and ferns.

Look out for the path on the right for Jenny Noble's Gill at the Buccleuch Estates sign and follow it as it climbs above the burn-hewn gully. Little is known of Jenny Noble; all that history – or, more accurately, hearsay – has recorded is that she was an old lady who is reputed to have hung herself here, leaving today's walkers with a name and a tantalisingly incomplete tale in a location of notable peace and tranquillity.

Cross the old railway line and take the path heading left uphill, turning left again when it rejoins the track from the outward route. Follow this back to the Round House, once a Victorian summer house but now bricked up into an inaccessible stone tower, albeit one with a great view over Langholm.

Continue past the tower on the woodland track, which then becomes a tarmac road. Where it then meets the main road back into Langholm, turn right and wander back to the start, enjoying the shops and cafés en route.

Potholm and Castle Hill

Distance 9.5km **Time** 3 hours
Terrain tracks, paths and open hill
Map OS Explorer 323 **Access** parking at
Kilngreen car park (free); buses
from Galashiels, Selkirk, Carlisle
and Lockerbie

**Follow in the footsteps of the brutal
Border Reivers on a far from shadowy
route of babbling rivers, bluebell-scented
woodland and open hillside complete
with lofty ridge-top views. Along the
way is a brace of man-made features,
including the remains of a once mighty
stronghold and a pretty cast-iron bridge.**

If visiting Langholm at the tail-end of
July take note of the annual Common
Riding festivities, a historic event in
which folk ride out on horseback to
inspect the town boundaries. Langholm's
is a particularly rousing affair with streets
resounding to the skirl of pipes and
drums, flag-waving pageantry and
cantering horses.

From the car park head away from the
town, briefly upstream along Ewes Water,
and across the river at Ewes Bridge. By the
pillars to the estate entrance and sawmill
go left through the wooden gates and
follow the path left around the field edge.

The scant remains of Langholm's
16th-century castle, purportedly built by
members of the Armstrong clan, stand at
the meeting of the rivers Ewes and Esk.
The Armstrongs held sway in this area
during the time of the bloody Border
skirmishes when Langholm fell under the
uncertain jurisdiction of the 'Debatable
Lands'. To ensure their survival some
border families turned to 'reiving'
– cattle rustling, plundering, kidnapping –
at which the Armstrongs succeeded
better than most. Scotland's James V
saw them as such a threat that he tricked
one of their most infamous leaders,
Johnnie Armstrong of Gilnockie, into a
meeting and had him and 36 of his
followers hanged as an example to other
freebooters who flouted his law.

Follow the path along the bank of the

◄ Ewes Bridge

River Esk, passing the elegant Duchess Bridge – assumed to be in honour of the Duchess of Buccleuch – cast in 1813 and the first of its kind in Scotland. Continuing on the path, pass the pheasant-rearing sheds, curve around to the right and then away from the river up to Holmhead Farm.

Follow the track to the left passing in front of the steading and on past North Lodge, staying with the main woodland track. After about 800m the woods thin out to reveal views of Potholm Farm and the Eskdale hills. At the track junction, by the wooden bench, take the left fork down the hill and pass above Potholm Farm to the T-junction.

Turn sharp right and follow the track as it meanders up the hill. Cross the stile and turn immediately right, following the line of the fence as it climbs up between Wrae Hass and Potholm Hill. Just before the brow of the ridge, take the stile on the right, cross the field and go over the next stile. Follow the drystane dyke up Potholm Hill, enjoying great views along the Ewes and Esk valleys and beyond.

Continue along the dyke as it leads down off the hill, over the ladder stile and then alongside a more robust dyke. Carry on straight ahead to climb to the summit

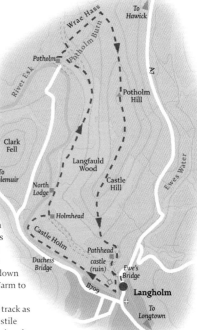

of Castle Hill, where this dyke bears sharply left.

There isn't an obvious path on the descent, simply head for Langholm through the scrubby hawthorn trees scattered across the hillside, eventually passing a footpath marker to join a rough track. Cross the ladder stile and carry on downhill to the lane, turn right passing Pathhead and returning to Ewes Bridge and back to town.

Warb Law

Distance 7km **Time** 2 hours
Terrain pavement, tracks and open hills
(this walk is unsuitable with dogs
March–May when calving cattle are on
the hills) **Map** OS Explorer 323
Access parking at Kilngreen car park
(free); buses from Galashiels, Selkirk,
Carlisle and Lockerbie

**Start along the pretty River Esk to strike
out over boggy and bracken-clad hillside
for the climb to the summit of Warb Law,
where all the puffing is rewarded with
fine panoramic views.**

Pretty Langholm nestles cosily below
the confluence of the River Esk and Ewes
Water, joined by Wauchope Water a little
further south. It was thanks to this
abundance of water that Langholm's
historic fortunes were transformed by the
many tweed mills that were established
along the riverbanks. The first mill was
built in 1789 and numerous others
followed over the next century. Today the
big mills have gone but Langholm is not
without a creative streak. As well as being
home to artists and jewellery-makers, the
town has continued associations with
weaving and cloth and a number of
smaller specialist textile producers are
located around the town.

Leaving the car park turn right and then
first right over the River Esk, then left
along Elizabeth Street. On the Esk's west
bank lies Langholm's 'new town', largely
built during the late 18th century,
coinciding with the growth of the textile
industry. Follow the road sharp right

passing the parish church, built in 1842 complete with a fine hammer-beam roof, and turn left on over the footbridge into Buccleuch Park.

Head straight across the park and on to Easton's Walk, an attractive woodland footpath that follows the course of the river. Go left at the path junction to stay with the river, passing alongside grassland eventually to meet the main A7 road. During late summer, this stretch is a mass of swirling sand martins frantically feeding and building up reserves before their long migration south. Go right at the main road and after about 50m take the little footpath uphill through the trees. Turn right onto the track following it as it curves left up to the open hillside.

Just after the farm sheds, leave the track and climb steeply up the open hillside following the row of pylons rising uphill at right angles to the track. Depending on the time of year, you might have to follow your nose as there isn't a clear path. In winter it can be boggy underfoot, while in summer it can be thick with bracken. Just find the clearest-looking route up and press on through.

When the pylons veer diagonally right follow this line all the way to the transmitter at the top of Warb Law (also known as Warbla), from where there are panoramic views over the Langholm hills, along Ewes valley and south to the mountains of Cumbria.

Descend the hill on the clearly defined track, staying with it as it sharply curves right then keeping ahead when another track branches off left. Go through the metal gate and along the beech-lined track, with the verge a purple haze of flowers in summer. At the cottage go straight ahead, on through a gap in the bushes and down the steps back into Buccleuch Park. From here retrace your steps back to the start.

◀ Warb Law above Langholm

Langholm town and burn

Distance 6km **Time** 2 hours
Terrain pavement, footpaths, and quiet
roads **Map** OS Explorer 323 **Access** parking
at Kilngreen car park (free); buses from
Galashiels, Selkirk, Carlisle and Lockerbie

For anyone less inclined to go scrambling
up the hills, this shorter route is a chance
to enjoy Langholm's fine riverside
location, historic buildings, accessible
countryside and sweeping hill views –
without the strenuous bits. The return
section includes a short loop to explore
Langholm's recent resurgence as an arts
town, from fine art to silversmithing.

Turn right out of the car park, then first
right to cross the River Esk, then
immediately right onto the riverside
Francis Street to pass behind the
Buccleuch Centre. Turn right again on

rejoining the main road and continue past
Langholm Academy and the Victorian
bowling green. Turn left opposite the
Sports Centre, right at the crossroads by
Douglas Terrace, and go up the steps
veering left to go into and through
Gala Side Wood.

On exiting the wood follow the track
uphill to the right, passing a well-
positioned bench with views of Whita Hill
and Scott's Knowe. Follow the track as it
veers left at the end of the houses,
passing numerous horse paddocks,
eventually giving way to a more uneven
and indistinct woodland path. At a
drystane dyke drop down to cross the
bridges over the babbling waters of the
Becks Burn. This is an irresistible spot for
a paddle on a warm summer's day. On
leaving head steeply up the other side and

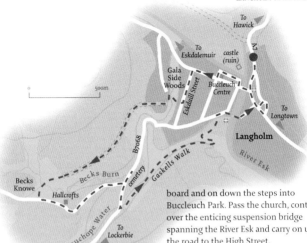

turn left along the winding lane until it joins the main road.

At the road take a short detour left to Langholm cemetery, crammed full of interesting, higgledy-piggledy gravestones, many carved with icons of local trades. Retrace your steps and carry on over the stone bridge spanning Wauchope Water, then taking Gaskells Walk on the left. This beautiful path rises above the carved ravine of the gushing waters below; look out for the gravestones in the cemetery on the opposite bank, some now hanging precariously close to the edge.

The path curves away from the water and fine views of Langholm and the surrounding hills open up ahead. Go left at the Hill Farm wildlife information board and on down the steps into Buccleuch Park. Pass the church, continue over the enticing suspension bridge spanning the River Esk and carry on up the road to the High Street.

To return to the start go left; alternatively turn right for a short tour of Langholm. Behind the Town Hall, built in 1811 on the site of the old tolbooth, stop to admire the old carved doorway made by locally-born and raised, 'godfather of civil engineering', Thomas Telford. Next to this is an information board commemorating astronaut Neil Armstrong's visit to Langholm to explore his clan heritage.

After the garage turn left up Drove Road, passing the converted church which is now a studio and gallery. Turn left at the road junction, but first look up to the top of the steep hill to Arkinholm Terrace, birthplace of poet Hugh MacDiarmid. Once back at the High Street turn right and wander along to the start, enjoying the temptations of the numerous cafés, galleries and independent shops along the way.

◀ The River Esk at Langholm

Byre Burn and the Fairy Loup

Distance 3.5km Time 1 hour 30
Terrain woodland footpath, farm track
and quiet roads Map OS Explorer 323
Access parking at the woodland
information point around 500m north of
Canonbie Bridge on the Byreburnfoot
road on the eastern side of the River Esk;
bus from Langholm, Annan and Carlisle

The Byre Burn rises north of the village
of Canonbie and flows south to join the
River Esk on its way to the Solway Firth.
This short loop begins on the east bank
of the Esk, towards Byreburnfoot, with
mixed woodland, commercial plantation
and river views. A short but steep climb
early on will get the heart pumping, but
after that it's a gentle stroll all the way.

From the parking lay-by, cross the road
and enter the woods. Go straight on for
around 50m and, where the hill starts to
climb, take the left-hand path through the
woods. At a waymarker, bear left to cross

a small bridge. Keep ahead through the
trees to cross another bridge, beyond
which follow the path as it contours left
around the base of a hill.

After about 80m, where a gravel path
joins from the left, continue ahead.
Follow the path along the base of the hill
until it starts rising to the right, with
steps then rising steeply. Climb the steps
and pause for a moment at the top to
enjoy the view of the valley behind and
hills rolling to the east, with the sawmill
below. A well-placed bench here at the top
of the steps makes a good spot for a rest.

Continue ahead on the path from the
bench before following a field boundary,
first to the left and then right as
waymarked. Where the path meets a track,
head left to reach the road. It was here
that the Byreburn railway viaduct
spanned the gorge below, part of the
North British Railway company's
Langholm Line opened in 1864.